GONE UNDER

2ND EDITION

Historic Cemeteries of Nashville, Tennessee

Mark Zimmerman

Zimco Publications LLC

Gone Under: Historic Cemeteries of Nashville, Tennessee – 2nd Edition
Copyright © 2012, 2019 Mark Zimmerman
Zimco Publications LLC
Website: zimcopubs.com
Email: info@zimcopubs.com

ISBN: 978-0-9858692-4-3

All rights reserved.

All Text, Photographs, and Maps by the Author Unless Otherwise Noted

No part of this book may be reproduced or transmitted in any form or by any means — electronic or manual, including photocopy, scanner, email, CD or other information storage and retreival system — without written permission from the author, except for personal use or as provided to the news media and book sellers.

Printed in the United States of America.

The text in this book, which is published to inform and entertain, should be used for general information and not as the ultimate source of educational or travel information. Many of the destinations listed in this book can be found on the Internet with the latest relevent information. Every effort has been made to ensure the accuracy and relevence of information in this book but the author and publisher do not assume responsibility for any errors, inaccuracies, omissions or inconsistencies within. Any slights of people, places, or organizations are strictly unintentional.

The names of organizations and destinations mentioned in this book may be trade names or trademarks of their owners. The author and publisher disclaims any connection with, sponsorship by or endorsement of such owners.

Also by Mark Zimmerman:

Guide to Civil War Nashville – 2nd Edition

God, Guns, Guitars & Whiskey: An Illustrated Guide to Historic Nashville, Tennessee – 2nd Edition

GONE UNDER
2nd Edition
Historic Cemeteries of Nashville, Tennessee

With the Appreciation of a Grateful Nation

Middle Tennessee State Veterans Cemetery
7931 McCrory Lane • Nashville, TN • (615) 532-2238

President Andrew Jackson 4
President James K. Polk..6
Historic Gravesites 7
Funeral for the Unknown Civil War Soldier......................9
Nashville City Cemetery...10
Mount Olivet Cemetery..20
Calvary Catholic Cemetery...32
Mount Ararat Cemetery (Greenwood West)...................33
Map of Cemeteries Southeast of Downtown 33
Greenwood Cemetery...34
Temple Jewish Cemetery 36
Mill Creek Baptist Church Cemetery 37
Nashville National Cemetery..38
Spring Hill Cemetery..46
Woodlawn Memorial Gardens 54
Forest Lawn Memorial Gardens.......................................60
Luton's Church (Grandpa Jones) 62
Hermitage Memorial Gardens..63
Harpeth Hills Memory Gardens.......................................64
Mount Hope Cemetery...64
Williamson Memorial Gardens 64
Hendersonville Memory Gardens.....................................65
Index of Burials by Name 66

President Andrew Jackson
The General and Beloved Wife Rachel Buried at The Hermitage Tomb

Andrew Jackson, the seventh President of the United States and the hero of the Battle of New Orleans, is entombed in the garden of his 1,120-acre estate The Hermitage, 12 miles east of downtown Nashville. The estate, Tennessee's most famous historic site, is a National Historic Landmark preserved by The Ladies Hermitage Association since 1889.

Jackson built the Greek-inspired tomb, designed by architect David Morrison, for his beloved wife Rachel, who died in 1828 just before he assumed the Presidency. The love affair between Andrew and Rachel Jackson burned bright throughout their marriage. Rachel was the daughter of John Donelson, one of the founders of Nashville. Jackson was buried at the tomb upon his death in 1845. A small family cemetery lies nearby. The garden was designed by Englishman William Frost in 1819 and features plants and shrubs of the early 19th Century.

Nearby is the cemetery of the Confederate Soldiers Home (non-extant) and the Donelson family.

During the presidential campaign of 1828, Jackson's opponents pointed to the Jacksons' marriage of August 1791. Rachel Donelson had been married to Lewis Robards of Kentucky, who mistreated her. She returned to her family in Nashville while Robards petitioned for a divorce. Convinced that Robards had obtained such a decree, Jackson took Rachel to Natchez and they were married. The divorce decree was not actually granted until 1793, and when the Jacksons learned of this discrepancy they remarried in Nashville in 1794.

Nothing much was mentioned of this incident until a newspaperman aligned with incumbent President John Quincy Adams printed the allegations that Rachel Donelson Jackson was an adultress. Others were much more scathing, calling her a whore and a "dirty, black wench." Jackson was wounded in the heart and fought against his impulse to lash back at his accusers. "The day of retribution and vengeance must come, when the guilty will meet with their just reward," he vowed.

Jackson won the 1828 election handily and he prepared to travel to Washington City for the inauguration. He knew that Rachel hated to travel, loved her life at The Hermitage, and hated Washington and politics. Although resigned to go with her husband, Rachel was sick at heart. On December 18, 1828, Rachel suffered a heart attack and died three days later. Jackson was inconsolable and the body of his wife literally had to be pried from his arms for burial. She was buried in the Hermitage garden. "At the time when I least expected it, and could least spare her, she was snatched from me," Jackson later wrote, "and I left here a solitary monument of grief, without the least hope of happiness here below."

Jackson's life had been punctuated by hard times. His father died before he was born, and by the age of 14 Jackson was an orphan. During the Revolutionary War he was struck on the arm and on the head by an angry British swordsman. He was forced to walk home miles in the rain, sick on his feet, and took months to recover from the disease that had killed his brother.

A descendant of the Scots-Irish, Jackson was a fighter and a resolute defender of his most precious commodity—his honor. He dueled with Charles Dickinson, a crack shot, over the ramifications of a proposed horse race. They met over the state line in Kentucky, with pistols at eight paces, in the early morning. Jackson held his fire by design. Dickinson

HERE LIE THE REMAINS OF
Mrs. RACHEL JACKSON
wife of PRESIDENT JACKSON
who died the 22nd Dec 1828-
Aged 61

Her face was fair, her person pleasing: her temper amiable, and her heart kind; she delighted in relieving the wants of her fellow creatures and cultivated that divine pleasure by the most liberal and unpretending methods: to the poor she was a benefactor; to the rich an example; to the wretched a comforter, to the prosperous an ornament, her piety went hand in hand with her benevolence, and she thanked her creator for being permitted to do good. A being so gentle, and yet so virtuous, slander might wound but could not dishonour; Even death, when he tore her from the armes of her husband, could but transport her to the bosom of her God.

fired first, hitting Jackson in the breast. Jackson wavered but stood his ground. He then fired but the pistol refused to discharge. It had only been half-cocked. Jackson fully cocked it and fired a bullet into Dickinson's abdomen. Dickinson bled to death before the day was out. The bullet in Jackson had missed his heart by an inch. It was too dangerous to try to remove it. When Jackson died, many years later in 1845, some speculated it was due to lead poisoning from the bullet he carried with him all those years.

In 1813, Jackson and several relatives engaged in a gunfight at Nashville's City Hotel with brothers Thomas Hart Benton and Jesse Benton. Jackson was hit in the left shoulder and arm. Weak from the loss of blood, Jackson fought off the doctors intending to amputate his damaged arm. The Benton brothers wisely left town.

In May 1833 on a riverboat excursion President Jackson was assaulted by distraught former naval officer Robert Randolph, who leaped at Jackson and bloodied his face. Jackson's nephew, Andrew Donelson, intervened. Two years later, Jackson was leaving a funeral service for a congressman when a young man leaped from the crowd near the Capitol rotunda and aimed a pistol at the President, only eight feet away. The cap ignited but the gunpowder did not. Jackson charged the would-be assassin with his walking stick. Richard Lawrence, an unemployed house painter, dropped the pistol and produced a second one, but it also misfired. Jackson had to be restrained from beating the man to death. Later, both guns were test-fired and found to be perfectly functional. The odds of both misfiring was tagged at 125,000 to one. Jackson claimed that the assassination attempt was the doings of a political foe, Senator George Poindexter, but Lawrence was found to be insane, having claimed to be the King of England and having once tried to kill his sister.

Jackson died at age 78 on Sunday, June 8, 1845 at The Hermitage. He passed before Sam Houston, whom he considered a son, could reach the estate for one last word. Jackson's last words were "What is the matter with my dear children? Have I alarmed you? Oh, do not cry. Be good children and we will all meet in Heaven."

Three thousand people attended the funeral. The Reverend John Todd Edgar officiated the service from the mansion's front portico. He read the 90th Psalm and all sang "How Firm a Foundation, Ye Saints of the Lord," one of Rachel's favorites. Jackson was laid to rest in the garden tomb next to Rachel. Reportedly a visitor to The Hermitage later asked one of the slaves if he thought Jackson had gone to heaven. "If the General wants to go," he replied, "who's going to stop him?"

In his last year of life Jackson received an interesting proposition. While in the Middle East, Commodore Jesse Elliott had obtained a marble Roman sarcophagus (tomb) thought to have held the remains of the Roman emperor Alexander Severus. He shipped it to the United States. He suggested that Jackson be buried in it when he died. Jackson wrote back: "I cannot consent that my mortal body be laid in a repository prepared for an Emperor or King—my republican feelings and principles forbid it—the simplicity of our system of government forbids it. Every monument erected to perpetuate the memory of our heroes and statesmen ought to be evidence of the economy and simplicity of our republican citizens, who are the sovereigns of our glorious Union, and whose virtue is to perpetuate it. True virtue cannot exist where pomp and parade are the governing passions. It can only dwell with the people...

"I have prepared a humble depository for my mortal body beside that wherein my beloved wife, where, without any pomp or parade, I have requested, when my God calls me to sleep with my fathers, to be laid, for both of us there to remain until the last trumpet sounds to call the dead to judgment, when we, I hope, shall rise together, clothed with that heavenly body promised to all who believe in our glorious Redeemer, who died for us that we might live, and by whose atonement I hope for a blessed immortality."

The Tennessee Confederate Soldiers' Home, completed in 1892 on 475 acres of The Hermitage, served 700 old soldiers during its 41 years of operation. It was demolished in 1953. Five hundred of the home's residents are buried in the Confederate Cemetery. The inscription on the stone monument reads in part: "This stone will stand the test of time. The souls of the tried men grouped about it will endure throughout eternity."

The remains of 60 slaves discovered at unmarked cemeteries at the nearby Ingleside and Cleveland Hall plantations have been reinterred at The Hermitage on grounds known as *Our Peace: Follow the Drinking Gourd*, a monument/sculpture designed by Tennessee professor Aaron Lee Benson. The sculpture consists of boulders arranged in a circle enclosing a straight stone wall marking the graves. Oak trees were placed to designate the Little Dipper constellation and the North Star. When runaway slaves traveled north to freedom in the early 1800s they sang the song *Follow the Drinking Gourd*, the "gourd" being the Little Dipper, which points to the North Star, their beacon.

President James K. Polk
Tomb at Tennessee State Capitol Holds 11th President and Wife Sarah

At the Tennessee State Capitol in downtown Nashville, just north of the Jackson Garden, is the tomb of James Knox Polk, the eleventh President of the United States, and Mrs. Sarah Childress Polk.

James K. Polk was born on Nov. 2, 1795 in Mecklenburg County, N.C., the eldest of ten children. He settled in Tennessee in 1818 after graduating from the University of North Carolina. The James K. Polk Ancestral Home in Columbia, Tenn. is a national shrine. As a teenager he survived a brutal backwoods gallstone operation which probably left him unable to conceive; he and his wife had no children.

Polk, the original "dark horse" candidate and a protégé of Andrew Jackson, served only one term (1845-49) as President but expanded the territory of the U.S. more than any other President. He may have been the hardest working President ever, working late into the night on many occasions. Reticent and sober, he had few friends, and sought and trusted his wife's advice on many matters.

Polk entered the Presidency with four goals—reduce the tariff, establish an independent Treasury, resolve the Oregon question, acquire California—and promised to serve only one term. He was true to his promises, accomplishing all four goals, and left office in 1849. But the duties of President had taken a terrible toll on his health, which was not good to begin with. He suffered from abdominal pains and chronic diarrhea. "I feel exceedingly relieved that I am now free of all public cares," he stated upon leaving office. Immediately after leaving the White House, James and Sarah Polk began a one-month journey down the East Coast, across Georgia and Alabama by rail, and then up the Mississippi to the Ohio and Cumberland rivers, then home to Nashville. The previous year the Polks had bought the home of famous lawyer Felix Grundy, a Polk mentor, not far from the new State Capitol. They renamed it Polk Place and began renovations and furnishings. The river and rail trip, with celebrations and honorary duties at each stop, exhausted the Polks. Several passengers on their steamship died of cholera. Rumors persisted that New Orleans was infected. The Polks arrived in Nashville on April 2, 1849 and soon thereafter occupied Polk Place. His health failed and he suffered for two weeks before dying on June 15th. His last words were "I love you, Sarah, for all eternity, I love you." Shortly before death he was baptized as a Methodist; his mother, still alive, had always wanted him to be baptized as a Presbyterian. He had the shortest retirement of all the Presidents, and died at age 54. As a suspected victim of cholera, Polk was buried in common grounds at the City Cemetery. Shortly thereafter,

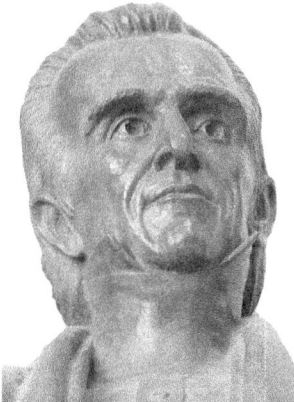

Polk Bust at State Capitol.

> The mortal remains of JAMES KNOX POLK are resting in the vault beneath. He was born in Mecklenburg County, North Carolina, and emigrated with his father, Samuel Polk, to Tennessee in 1806. The beauty of virtue was illustrated in his life. The excellence of Christianity was exemplified in his death. By his public policy he defined, established and extended the boundaries of his Country. He planted the laws of the American Union on the shores of the Pacific. His influence and his Counsels united to organize the National Treasury on the principles of the Constitution, and to apply the rule of Freedom to Navigation, Trade and Industry.

he was reinterred to a tomb at Polk Place designed by state capitol architect William Strickland. Sarah Childress Polk lived for another 42 years, dressing in black and rarely leaving Polk Place. As the widow of a President and grand dame of Nashville, dignitaries called on her with hat in hand, including many Union generals during the Civil War. When Sarah Polk died in 1891 she was buried beside her husband. The inscription on her tomb reads: "A noble woman, a devoted wife, a true friend, a sincere Christian." Despite instructions in his will that Polk Place be given to the State of Tennessee, the heirs sold it and it was demolished in 1901. The Polk Tomb was moved to the State Capitol grounds, just north of the Andrew Jackson garden.

Historic Gravesites

Counterclockwise from Left:

• The gravesite of Granny White (Lucinda Wilson White) is located at Granny White Pike and Travelers Ridge Drive. Lucinda, age 60, and two grandsons walked 900 miles from North Carolina to Nashville in 1803. She put up a ginger cake stand and a tar pit for greasing wagon wheels. By 1812 Granny had managed to purchase 50 hillside acres. She was an innkeeper, housekeeper, weaver, and cook. She also made her own whiskey and cider. Business was so good she added onto the inn. In 1816 she died at the age of 73.

• General Thomas Overton (1753-1825) is buried near the Old Hickory Village triangle. Overton served in the Revolutionary War and was one of Jackson's seconds in his famous Kentucky pistol duel with Charles Dickinson. Thomas Overton lived at his Soldier's Rest estate here from 1804 until his death in 1825.

• The abandoned family mausoleum at Belle Meade Plantation. Mortal remains were moved to Mt. Olivet Cemetery.

• The family cemetery at Rock Castle, home of General Daniel Smith (1748-1818), in Hendersonville.

• The rockpile gravesite of Kasper (Casper) Mansker (1750-1820) is located on Memorial Drive near French Street. Mansker is known as Goodlettsville's "first citizen." A "long hunter," he erected a fort in 1780 on Mansker's Creek. He was a signer of the Cumberland Compact.

Historic Gravesites

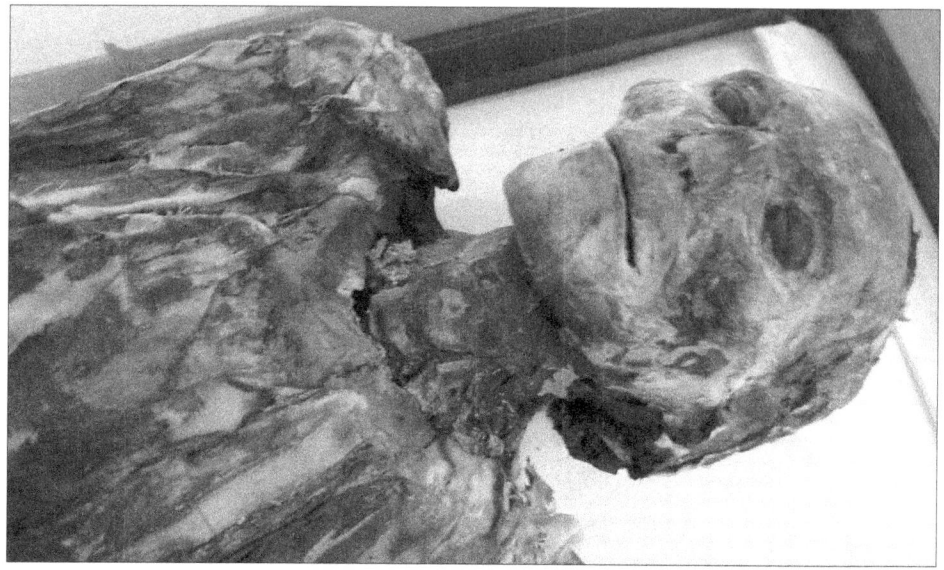

Clockwise from upper left:

• The gravesite of William Bowen (1742-1804) at the Bowen-Campbell House in Goodlettsville.

• The 3,500-year-old Egyptian mummy at the Tennessee State Museum.

• Bishop H.N. McTyeire tomb at Vanderbilt University.

• Mass grave marker for Tennessee Confederates at the McGavock Cemetery at Carnton Plantation in Franklin.

• Artillery overlooking the Stones River National Cemetery in Murfreesboro.

• Architect William Strickland's tomb at the Tennessee State Capitol.

Funeral for the Unknown Civil War Soldier

In May 2009 the remains of a Civil War soldier were found in a shallow grave near the site of the Battle of Franklin, uncovered during a construction project. Historians could not conclusively determine whether the soldier was Union or Confederate. Why the soldier was buried in a coffin south of Winstead Hill, away from others, has been an issue of contention.

The Battle of Franklin was fought on Nov. 30, 1864 between the Confederate forces of Gen. John Bell Hood and the Union forces of Gen. John Schofield. More than 2,000 were killed and 12 Confederate generals became casualties as the Army of Tennessee rashly attacked the fortified Union positions south of the town.

In October 2009, the unknown soldier's remains were laid to rest at Rest Haven Cemetery in Franklin following viewings and services at the antebellum St. Paul's Episcopal Church. A lengthy procession of blue and gray re-enactors and grieving women dressed in black accompanied the horse-drawn funeral carriage through the public square and into the cemetery, witnessed by hundreds of spectators and the media.

Among those attending were Harold Becker, 93,

of Grand Rapids, Mich., the son of Union veteran Charles Conrad Becker, who fought at the Battle of Franklin with the 128th Indiana Infantry; James Brown Sr., 97, of Knoxville, Tenn., whose father, James H.H. Brown of the 8th Georgia Infantry, saw his regiment cut in half at Gettysburg; and Corinne Davenport, whose father, Henry Clay Smith, fought with the 4th Tenn. Regiment and with Gen. Nathan Bedford Forrest. After the custom-made coffin bearing the unknown soldier was lowered into the ground at the gravesite marked with stone columns from the original state capitol, representatives walked to the open grave and sprinkled soil from the 18 states which had fought at the Battle of Franklin.

City Cemetery Walking Tour Map
Enter at Gate on 4th Avenue South and Oak Street

CITY CEMETERY
EST. 1822

Final Resting Place of the Founders and Notables

The Nashville City Cemetery at 1001 Fourth Avenue South and Oak Street opened in 1822 as the city's first public cemetery. It is the oldest public cemetery in Middle Tennessee. The previous burial grounds had been located at the public square and the Sulphur Spring Bottom.

Originally four acres, the cemetery was expanded gradually to its 27 acres. Alpha Kingsley, a captain in the U.S. Army and owner of a boarding house, laid out the cemetery grounds and served as the first sexton from 1822-46. Assisting him was Mrs. Louisa Grundy McGavock.

City Cemetery is laid out with streets and street signs much like a miniature city. Some of the streets can be driven but are very narrow (no tour buses are allowed inside the cemetery). There are numerous monuments and crypts to examine, and interpretive signage tells visitors much about the persons buried here. City Cemetery is open daily, 9-5; gates are locked dusk to dawn. A list of rules and regulations are posted near the administration building.

Among the 20,000 persons buried at City Cemetery are four of Nashville's founders (James and Charlotte Robertson and John and Ann Robertson Cockrill), four Confederate generals (Felix Zollicoffer, Bushrod Johnson, Richard Ewell, and Samuel Read Anderson), the man who named the American flag Old Glory (Captain William Driver), Union Navy Commodore Paul Shirley, Tennessee Governor William Carroll, 15 mayors of Nashville, and two of the original Fisk Jubilee Singers (Mabel Lewis Imes and Ella Sheppard Moore).

During the Civil War more than 14,000 soldiers were taken to Nashville's 25 military hospitals, which served much of the Western Theater. W.R. Cornelius was the official undertaker in Nashville and buried soldiers from both sides in the open field southwest of the cemetery. After the war, the U.S. soldiers were moved to National Cemetery and many of the Southerners were moved to Mount Olivet Cemetery.

Neglected over time, the cemetery was declared a public nuisance. In 1868, a local newspaper called the cemetery a ruin—"robbery, murder and lust have held their horrid orgies in it and even now nightly desecrated by being the rendezvous of lascivious love."

Preservation efforts at the cemetery over the years have been sporatic. After the Civil War, the newly opened Mount Olivet Cemetery, out in the countryside, became the place to be buried. Many burials at City Cemetery were relocated there. Calvary Catholic Cemetery opened alongside Mt. Olivet; Catholics had been buried in the southwest section of City Cemetery but the construction of railroad tracks cut the tract off from the main parcel, and the burials were reinterred. In 1879 squirrels were released to control the growth of oak trees, and ten years later a wire fence was erected from remnants of the condemned Cumberland River suspension bridge. Restorations occurred in 1946 and 1958.

The Nashville City Cemetery Association has actively been working to restore the City Cemetery and provide information about the burials there. In 2007 the Nashville City Council appropriated $3 million for renovations. Tombstones, markers, and vaults have been repaired and cleaned, the roads repaved, new lighting and restrooms installed. The Keeble administration building has been renovated. Working with the NCCA are the Metro Historical Commission and Master Gardeners of Davidson County.

A Living History Tour of the cemetery is conducted by the NCCA each fall. A wealth of information can be found at www.thenashvillecitycemetery.org.

Nashville's Oldest Burial Ground

The monument to Nancy Maynor, wife of painter Pleasant Maynor, was designed by Prussian immigrant Adolphus Heiman, one of Nashville's best-known architects. The monument was one of his first Nashville commissions. A butterfly graces the monument, which shows the signature A. Heiman.

The rock and lantern monument to Ann Rawlins Sanders, who died in 1836 at the age of 21. There is a romantic legend that she committed suicide after a lover's quarrel, and her lover marked her grave with a stone and a lantern, because of her fear of the dark. There is no explanation how this false legend began.

General Bushrod Rust Johnson was a professor at Nashville's Western Military Institute before the Civil War. His wife was buried at City Cemetery in 1858. During the war, he was captured at Fort Donelson, and was the hero at the Battle of Chickamauga, leading Longstreet's troops through the gap in the Union lines. He was buried in his native Ohio upon his death in 1880. In the 1970s his remains were reburied at City Cemetery with full military honors. He now lies beside his wife.

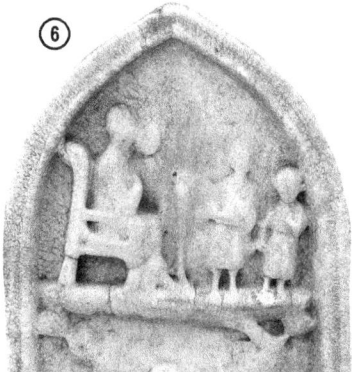

School teacher Pamelia Kirk's tombstone depicts a seated teacher and her pupils.

The monument of William Carroll (1788-1844), a Pennsylvania native and successful Nashville businessman who served longer than any other man as Tennessee's governor. As successor to Andrew Jackson as leader of Tennessee's militia, he was instrumental in victories against the Creek Indians at Horseshoe Bend in 1814 and against the British at New Orleans in 1815. In 1819 he brought the first steamboat, the *General Jackson*, to Nashville. As governor he was known as a "champion of the people" and the first governor to lead the General Assembly in issues of reform.

① **Samuel Read Anderson** (1804-1883) was a native Virginian and son of a Revolutionary War veteran. He served as Lieutenant Colonel of the "Bloody First" Tennessee Regiment in the Mexican War and as Nashville postmaster, 1853-61. During the Civil War he served as a Confederate Brigadier General under Gen. Robert E. Lee and successfully led his brigade at Cheat Mountain, Va. He then served under Magruder at Yorktown but his health faltered. He was appointed by CSA President Jefferson Davis to the Confederate Bureau of Conscription for Tennessee. Due to Union occupation, he had to operate this office out of Selma, Ala. He returned to Nashville after the war and prospered as a businessman.

② **J.D. Hill Family Vault** anchors the fenced oval area fronting the administration building.

③ **Marker–Revolutionary War Veterans** buried in the cemetery are Colonel Joel Lewis, John Bradford, Anthony Foster, Henry Marlin, Major John Cockrill, Samuel Chapman, Archibald Marlin, and Lipscomb Norvell.

④ **Nancy Maynor** (born in 1788) died in 1836, only eight years after marrying painter Pleasant Maynor. Her monument was designed by Prussian émigré and noted architect Adolphus Heiman. It was one of his first commissions in Nashville. It is marked with a butterfly.

⑤ **Captain William Driver Flag Pole** displays the American flag in honor of the retired sea captain and Nashville resident (buried in this cemetery) who named his ship's flag Old Glory.

⑥ **Pamelia A. Kirk** (1780-1860) was the first woman school teacher in Nashville. She was a native of Virginia. Her headstone carving depicts a teacher and her young students.

⑦ **Ann Rawlins Sanders** (born in 1815) died in 1836 at the age of 21, only four years after marrying Charles Sanders. She is buried near the boulder monument topped with a lantern, reportedly because she was afraid of the dark. A devout member of the First Presbyterian Church, her obituary said she was "a woman whose piety made her celestial among mortals." Legend says she committed suicide after a lover's quarrel but this is false. Ann Sanders was buried on the lot of Edward Steele, who probably was her brother-in-law. Her box tomb is near the boulder. Sexton Dan Marlin in 1902 claimed Marion Steele is buried under the boulder.

⑧ **Mayor Raphael Benjamin "Ben" West** (1911-1974) served as Mayor of Nashville from 1951 to 1963. He favored desegregation of public facilities, presided over one of the first federal urban renewal projects, and unsuccessfully opposed city-county consolidation in the early 1960s. In 1958 Mayor West led a major restoration project for the City Cemetery.

⑨ **Marker–Mayors of Nashville** lists all the mayors of Nashville and those who are buried at City Cemetery—20, including first mayor Joseph Coleman (1806-08) and son Thomas (1842).

⑩ **General William Carroll** (1788-1844), a native of Pittsburgh, Pa., commanded militia under Gen. Andrew Jackson during the Creek War and at the Battle of New Orleans in 1815. He was severely wounded at the Battle of Horseshoe Bend. He had come to Nashville in 1810 at age 22. He owned a hardware store and nail factory. He brought the first steamboat, the *General Jackson,* to Nashville. He served six terms as governor, longer than any other. He served as a champion of the common man against the interests of the wealthy, a precursor for Jackson's subsequent political conquests. The State of Tennessee erected his monument, complete with military regalia. Carroll County, Tenn. is named for him.

⑪ **Bushrod Rust Johnson** (1817-1880) was a native of Ohio, a Quaker by faith, a West Point graduate, and instructor at Western Military Institute in Nashville. In 1858 he buried his wife Martha here. He served with distinction in the Confederate Army, best known for leading the charge through the broken Union line at the Battle of Chickamauga in 1863. He was severely wounded at Shiloh. He died in 1880 in Ohio. In the 1970s he was brought to Nashville to rest beside his wife, buried with a military service, including a 21-gun salute with black gunpowder rifles.

⑫ **Marker–General James Rains** of a prominent Nashville family was killed at the Battle of Murfreesboro (Stones River) on Dec. 31, 1862. He was buried here first but he has since been reinterred at Mount Olivet Cemetery.

⑬ **Andrew Ewing** (1740-1813) was a signer of the Cumberland Compact and the first clerk of the County Court or Committee of the Notables. Raised as a Quaker, Ewing brought his wife and six children to Nashville from Pennsylvania. His son, Nathan, succeeded him as clerk.

⑭ **Judge Robert Whyte** (1767-1844) was a Judge of the Supreme Court of Errors and Appeals and a Masonic high officer.

⑮ **John Kane** was a stonecutter who worked on the construction of the State Capitol. He died of consumption in 1848. His monument was designed by capitol architect William Strickland of Philadelphia. The tools of the stonecutter's trade are carved in stone atop the monument. The stone came from the same quarry supplying the capitol construction.

⑯ **Sarah Ann Gray Walker**'s monument is the other work of Strickland's at City Cemetery. She was a Florence, Ala. native and the wife of John W. Walker. She died in 1845 at the age of 28. The Roman arch protects the lachrymal vase (a copy of those found in the ruins of Pompeii) and supports a torch on top. It is constructed of pure white marble from Baltimore.

⑰ **Charles Maddis** was Gen. Andrew Jackson's interpreter at the Battle of New Orleans. A Frenchman originally named Longonotti, he died in a house fire in 1854 along with his two young grandsons, who are buried beside him.

⑱ **Mary Cannon Bryan** was the daughter of Governor Newton Cannon and wife of businessman W.P. Bryan. She died at the age of 24 in 1848 of nervous affliction. Legend has it that W.P. Bryan's second wife, Josephine, whom he married in 1860, had the grave-

The Rutledge Monument features the likeness of a palmetto tree from their native South Carolina.

The tomb of John Kane "erected by the Stonecutters of the State House." He was head of the crew of stonecutters for the State Capitol. This massive monolith designed by capitol architect William Strickland features an egg-and-dart cornice and limestone carvings of the tools of the stone mason.

The Baxter-Watkins Monument is an ornate spire.

The tomb of Sarah Ann Gray Walker, designed by William Strickland in 1845, features a Roman arch with egg-and-dart moulding, scrolls with acanthus volutes, a dentil cornice, and laurel wreath and torch with flame. The vase is a copy of those found in the ruins of Pompeii. Mrs. Walker was 28 years old at the time of her death.

This slender cenotaph extolls the accomplishments of John Sevier, Tennessee's first governor. Sevier is buried in Knoxville, Tenn.

stone epitaph removed, but there is no evidence an epitaph was ever inscribed. During the Civil War, the Bryans lived on his Alabama plantation and then in France.

(19) Major Henry Rutledge (1775-1844) was the son of Edward Rutledge, a signer of the Declaration of Independence. He married Septima Sexta Middleton (1783-1865), the daughter of Arthur Middleton, another signer. They were from Charleston, S.C. and were cousins. Septima Sexta's name refers to the fact that she was the sixth daughter and seventh child of her parents. Their family home, Middleton Place, was famous for its formal gardens. Henry Rutledge owned 50,000 acres in Franklin County, Tenn., an inheritance from his father's Revolutionary War land grant. They had a summer home there and a town home, Rose Hill, in Nashville. Septima Sexton helped charter the Christ Church Episcopal in Nashville.

(20) Francis B. Fogg (1795-1880) was a Nashville lawyer and Christ Church vestryman who married Mary Rutledge (1801-1872), daughter of Henry and Septima Sexta Rutledge. He was one of three men who developed the first public school system for Nashville. An advanced high school, Hume-Fogg on Broadway, is named for him and Alfred Hume, who is also buried at City Cemetery. Mary Rutledge Fogg and her mother helped establish the House of Industry for young destitute women and the Protestant Orphan Asylum. She was the author of seven books, including a science textbook used as a standard college text. Their only surviving child, Henry, was killed at the Battle of Fishing Creek, Ky. in early 1862.

(21) W.A. Johnson Family Vault is one of only four above-ground vaults at the City Cemetery.

(22) John Sevier Cenotaph is a monument to the first Tennessee governor, pioneer, war hero, Indian fighter, and Congressman. Sevier is buried at the Knoxville, Tenn. courthouse.

(23) Robert Baxter and Watkins Monument. Robert Baxter was one of the pioneering iron masters in Middle Tennessee, owner of the Tennessee Iron Works in the 1830s. He was a partner of Anthony Van Leer. The monument bears the likeness of an ironworks.

(24) Thomas Claiborne (1780-1856). A native of Virginia, Claiborne was a lawyer who served in the Tennessee House of Representatives (1811-12). He was a major under Andrew Jackson during the Creek War. He also served as Mayor of Nashville and as the first Masonic Grand Master of F.& A.M. of Tennessee.

(25) William Edward West (1788-1857) was a talented artist who painted the famous portrait of Lord Byron and Shelley. Born in Lexington, Ky., he traveled to Europe and became a member of the Royal Academy. His best-known American work is that of Robert E. Lee in 1838, long before the Civil War. In ill health, he moved to Nashville to live with his sister Sarah and her husband Robert Woods.

(26) General Richard S. Ewell, also known as Old Baldy, led Stonewall Jackson's corps at Gettysburg after Jackson's death in 1863. He retired to Spring Hill, Tenn. after marrying Lizinka Campbell Brown (1820-1872), the daughter of George Washington Campbell (1768-1848), who was a congressman, senator, Secretary of the Treasury under President Madison, member of the Tennessee Supreme Court and Minister to Russia. Ewell and his wife both died in 1872. Campbell is also buried here.

(27) Educators Marker honors those buried here–teacher Pamelia Kirk; William Hume and Dr. C.D. Elliott, presidents of the Nashville Female Academy; Alfred Hume, founder of the Nashville public school system; Francis Fogg, first president of Nashville Board of Education; and Robert P. Curran, commissioner of public instruction.

(28) Alfred Hume (1808-1853) was one of the founders of Nashville's public school system. Hume School opened in 1855 with 12 teachers. Hume-Fogg High School on Broadway, built in 1912, is named for him. He was the son of William Hume, a native of Scotland who was the first minister at the First Presbyterian Church. His wife, Louisa, was the daughter of Revolutionary War veteran John Bradford, who is buried nearby. Louisa and her widowed sister Evelina worked as volunteer nurses in Nashville's military hospitals in the early days of the Civil War. Both caught pneumonia and died within days of each other.

(29) John McNairy Family Vault is the resting place of John McNairy (1762-1837), a friend of Andrew Jackson and a Superior Court Judge. He appointed Jackson as prosecuting attorney for Davidson County. He was appointed by President Washington as one of the three judges for the newly created Southwest Territory. He served on the convention which created the State of Tennessee and served on the first Superior Court. In 1797 President Washington named him to the U.S. District Court. He was known for upholding the spirit of the law and not just the letter of the law. He owned 11,000 acres in Davidson and Sumner counties, including his 477-acre farm Bellview. He and his wife had no children, but as the oldest brother he was responsible for constructing the family vault. Legend places robbers and escaped Confederate prisoners in a cave beneath the monument. McNairy County, Tenn. is named for him.

(30) General James Robertson (1742-1814) was the "Father of Middle Tennessee" and one of the original Nashville pioneers. He and wife Charlotte had eleven children. Two of their sons were killed by Indians. The seventh, son Felix, was the first white child born in the Cumberland settlements. Felix grew up to be Nashville mayor and a well-loved pediatrician. He and his wife Lydia Waters of Philadelphia are buried here.

James Robertson, along with land speculator Judge Richard Henderson and colleague John Donelson, were responsible for leading settlers to lands along the Cumberland River where Nashville now stands. Earlier, native Virginian Robertson had been instrumental in establishing the Watauga settlements in Carolina territory west of the mountains (what is now Elizabethton, Tenn.).

After several preliminary trips to the Cumberland region with small parties, Robertson and his larger group of Watauagans arrived overland at the Nashville site in 1779 and became the first permanent white settlers. In his book *Winning of the West*, Teddy Roosevelt called Robertson's trek "being equal in importance to the settlement of Jamestown or the landing at Plymouth Rock."

Ten years later Robertson was appointed Lieutenant Colonel

The family burial plot of General James Robertson, the "Father of Middle Tennessee," wife Charlotte Robertson, and son Felix Robertson, the first white child born in the Cumberland settlements.

The monument of Captain William Driver was self-designed. The old sea captain's flag was known as Old Glory.

The monument and underground burial vault of the John McNairy family is the source of several legends, one being that escaped Confederate prisoners from nearby Fort Negley hid in the chamber underneath the monument.

Confederate General Richard S. Ewell of Virginia fought in the Eastern Theater, lost a leg at Second Manassas, and commanded Stonewall Jackson's old division at Gettysburg. In 1863, he married Lizinka C. Brown of Nashville and retired after the war to Spring Hill, Tenn., where he operated a prosperous farm.

Commandant of the Mero District of the Southwest Territory. The next year, President Washington named him brigadier general of the U.S. Army of that district.

Charlotte Robertson (1751-1843) was every bit as much the rugged pioneer as her husband. The city of Charlotte in Dickson County, Tenn. is named for her. She was the hero of the Battle of the Bluffs at Fort Nashborough in April 1781. When the men outside the fort were attacked by Indians, she released the hounds, which caused enough chaos that the men could safely retreat back into the stockade.

A stone monument to the Robertsons can be seen at Nashville's Centennial Park, near the Parthenon. A replica of their log house can be seen at H.G. Hill Park on Charlotte Pike in west Nashville.

Ann Robertson Johnston was Charlotte's widowed sister-in-law, who brought her three children with her on the historic Donelson riverboat journey to Nashville in 1780. She married fellow pioneer John Cockrill and resided where Centennial Park now stands. The Cockrills were reinterred at City Cemetery in 1911.

㉛ **Duncan Robertson** (1770-1833) was a bookseller, city alderman, philanthropist, doer of good deeds, and, according to his gravestone, "the best man that ever lived in Nashville." He was a native of Scotland. He died in 1833. He was not related to James Robertson.

㉜ **General Sam G. Smith** (1794-1835) was an aide to General Carroll at the Battle of New Orleans, a state senator, and Tennessee Secretary of State. His motto was "Office has no charms to justify a sacrifice of principle."

㉝ **Alex C. Brown** (1811-1830) was killed at age 19 during his duty as a fireman. Members of Nashville Fire Company No. 1 raised the funds to erect a monument to him in the shape of a fire hydrant.

㉞ **General Robert Armstrong** (1791-1854) was loved by Andrew Jackson as a son and assisted the general in many of his campaigns. Jackson presented his sword to him. He served as Postmaster, 1829-45, ran unsuccessfully for governor, and was appointed by President Polk as Consul to Liverpool. He married Margaret Nichol over the objections of her father. They eloped and were married at The Hermitage, home of Andrew and Rachel Jackson, who had also eloped. Jackson acted as peacemaker and invited all of the families to a reconciliation dinner. Margaret died in 1834.

㉟ **John E. Hagey** (1748-1841) was a Frenchman who came to America with General Lafayette and later became his bodyguard. He fought with the French Lighthorse at White Plains and Yorktown. He eventually became a U.S. citizen, married, and settled in Nashville. At age 77 he was in Huntsville, Ala. on business when he heard that Lafayette was to visit Nashville. He walked over 100 miles and arrived in Nashville during the grand parade in Lafayette's honor. The general recognized him and embraced his old friend. Hagey's military funeral was attended by five thousand people.

㊱ **Wilkins Tannehill** (1787-1858), a native of Pittsburgh, Pa., served as Mayor of Nashville in 1825-26, a Trustee of the University of Nashville, and as Masonic Grand High Priest of the Grand Royal Arch Chapter of Tennessee. He wrote the Masonic standard national manual, welcomed Lafayette and President Monroe to Nashville, and presided over the Masonic ceremonies at the laying of the State Capitol cornerstone.

㊲ **Ella Shepherd Moore** (1851-1914) was one of the original Jubilee Singers of Fisk University. The choral group toured the world singing Negro spirituals to raise money for their college, which was established for black students in Nashville following the Civil War.

㊳ **Civil War Burials.** Union and Confederate soldiers were buried in mass graves along the railroad tracks until after the war when the Union dead were moved to National Cemetery and the Confederates to Mount Olivet Cemetery.

㊴ **Thomas Crutcher** (1760-1844) of Virginia served as Mayor in 1819 and served as Treasurer of the State of Tennessee for 25 years. He was a trustee of the Nashville Female Academy, established in 1817. The inscription says he was "stern but virtuous."

㊵ **Commodore Paul Shirley** (1821-1876) of the U.S. Navy commanded the *Suwanee*, which carried 12 heavy guns and was capable of sailing both ways, a double-ender. He once sailed from San Francisco to Vancouver, British Columbia in four days. His brother, John, was a Confederate naval commander. Paul Shirley's marker states that he was an Admiral.

㊶ **Captain William Driver** (1803-1886) was a New England ship captain who sailed around the world twice, flying his homemade American flag he called Old Glory. He was famous for rescuing the descendants of the survivors of the *HMS Bounty* mutiny. Retiring to Nashville, Capt. Driver, a staunch Unionist who had several sons in the Confederate Army (one was killed in battle), flew Old Glory from the State Capitol when Union troops captured Nashville in February 1862. "I am now ready to die and go to my forefathers," he said after raising the flag. Subsequently, as soldiers relayed the story, the U.S. flag came to be known as Old Glory. He had hidden the flag from local secessionists after Tennessee entered the Confederacy by stitching it inside a bedcover. The captain's flag is now at the Smithsonian Institution in Washington, D.C. Captain Driver designed his own grave marker, which features an anchor and inscriptions. Due to Capt. Driver's presence, the City Cemetery is one of the few places authorized by Congress to fly the American flag 24 hours a day.

㊷ **General Felix Zollicoffer** (1812-1862) was a Nashville newspaper editor and Whig politician. In the 1830s he served as a lieutenant of volunteers in the Second Seminole War. He served in the U.S. House from 1852-59. In 1860, he supported the Constitutional Union Party and opposed secession. When Tennessee broke from the Union, however, he followed suit and was named a Confederate brigadier general. In 1861 Zollicoffer and untested troops were ordered to Knoxville to suppress Unionist sentiment in East Tennessee. At the Battle of Fishing Creek (Mill Springs), Ky. in January 1862 he was killed when he wandered into enemy lines. He was known to be near-sighted and was wearing a rain slicker at the time. He was the first Confederate general killed in the Western Theater. His six daughters walked in the funeral procession from the Capitol to the cemetery, along with his horse, which had been wounded in the ear.

Fireman Alex Brown's monument is shaped like a fire hydrant.

The monument at the gravesite of Ella Dallas is one of the few statues at the cemetery.

The gravesite of Harlan Howard, the dean of Nashville country music songwriters, who died in 2002 at age 74. A Civil War scholar, he was granted his wish to be buried near his hero, General Felix Zollicoffer.

The impressive crypt of Dr. John Selby and family features a gated stone and wrought-iron fence.

Mable Imes and Ella Shephard Moore were two of the original Jubilee Singers of Fisk University.

The monument of John Peabody, a Mason, shows the three styles of Greek-Roman columns (left to right) Doric, Ionic, and Corinthian.

43 Harlan Howard (1929-2002) was the "Dean of Nashville Songwriters," penning 4,000 songs over five decades and scoring more than one hundred hits in the Top Ten. His breakthrough hit was "Heartaches by the Number" by Ray Price in 1959. His best work was probably "I Fall to Pieces" sung by Patsy Cline, which he co-wrote with Hank Cochran. In the early 1960s he was named Billboard's Songwriter of the Year for two years running. His epitaph reads: "He wrote songs; I held the pen" and "Country Music–Three Chords and the Truth." He died in 2002. A Civil War scholar, his wish was to be buried near Gen. Zollicoffer, which was granted. He was married to country music entertainer Jan Howard.

44 White Turpin (1813-1865), a Mississippian in Darden's Battery of Hood's Army of Tennessee, died one month after being wounded at the Battle of Nashville. He was 22. His mother buried him away from the other soldiers.

45 Mable Lewis Imes (1858-1936) was one of the original Jubilee Singers of Fisk University. The choral group toured the world singing Negro spirituals to raise money for their college, which was established for black students in Nashville following the Civil War.

46 Ella Dallas was the wife of Triv B. Dallas and died in Pensacola, Fla. in 1873. Hers is one of the few monuments at City Cemetery to feature a statue.

47 John Peabody (1792-1850), a Mason, has a monument that features examples of the three types of Greek-Roman columns: Doric, Ionic, and Corinthian.

48 Feedrick Smith's simple tablet describes him as a sailor and the "first Rigger on Capital Hill." He died in 1848 at age 43. He and John Peabody are buried in the lot purchased by the Masonic Lodge, Cumberland #8, in the 1820s.

49 Ann Robertson Johnston Cockrill (1757-1821) came to Nashville with Donelson's 1780 flotilla. She was the widowed sister of General James Robertson and had three young daughters. She married fellow pioneer John Cockrill and they lived where Centennial Park now stands. She organized a school for the pioneer children and thus became Nashville's first school teacher. She also taught Nashville's first Sunday School class. The Cockrills' remains were moved from their family cemetery to City Cemetery in 1911. She is commemorated with a bronze plaque on a large granite stone in Centennial Park.

50 Ephraim Foster (1794-1854) served as Andrew Jackson's secretary during the Creek War. A lawyer, he served as Speaker of the Tennessee House of Representatives and as a U.S. Senator, 1843-45. He was the law partner of Francis Fogg. Foster & Fogg was known for helping slaves legally purchase their freedom. Foster was said to be a great orator, teller of jokes, and quick to anger.

51 Dr. John Shelby (1786-1859) was a physician who established the Shelby Medical College, which was destroyed during the Civil War. Shelby lost an eye in the Seminole War serving with General Jackson. He also served as postmaster. He served as president of the Tennessee Agricultural Society. He inherited most of what is now East Nashville from his father, David Shelby, an early settler and Revolutionary War veteran. Shelby Park is named for the family. The family vault contains John Shelby and wife Anna Mariah, mother Sarah Bledsoe Shelby, two daughters, two sons-in-law, a grandson and his wife.

52 Dr. Gerard Troost (1776-1850), a native of the Netherlands, served as the first state geologist from 1831-50. He helped conceive the railroad tunnel at Cowan, Tenn., and chose the site. From his arrival in Tennessee in 1827 until 1832 he operated the Nashville Museum of Natural History, where he displayed his artifacts, which eventually totaled 22,000. He was a science professor at the University of Nashville from 1828 to 1850. His private library exceeded 7,000 volumes. In Europe he was an M.D. and pharmacist. He managed the mineral collection of Louis Bonaparte in Paris. He was a protégé of Hauy, the father of crystallography. In 1810 he moved to Philadelphia, Pa., married, and served at the local College of Pharmacy. His wife died in 1819, leaving him with two small children. He remarried and moved to the New Harmony, Ind. commune.

53 Richard Love's gravestone features a hand pointing a finger toward heaven.

CITY OF THE DEAD

Mt. Olivet Cemetery

Mount Olivet Cemetery was created in 1856 to serve as the final resting place for Nashvillians after space at the Old City Cemetery had become limited. Today there are 190,000 people buried there, including many prominent local citizens. Visitors can view crypts, vaults, monuments, statues, cherubs, angels, maidens, Christ figures, interpretive signage, and a variety of funerary artwork on this hilltop Victorian-era cemetery. Located at 1101 Lebanon Road, two-and-a-half miles east of downtown, Mt. Olivet Cemetery is a modern facility with a historic past. Rules of decorum apply.

The Furman Monument is the largest in the cemetery, its eight columns depicted as caryatids—female figures similar to the Erechtheum's porch of maidens in Athens. The monument, which is 18 feet tall, was built by Mary J. Furman in honor of her late husband, Francis Furman (1816-99), a wealthy merchant. She also bequeathed money to Vanderbilt University to build Furman Hall in 1907. • At right is the Daniel Hillman monument.

Mount Olivet Cemetery Walking Tour Map

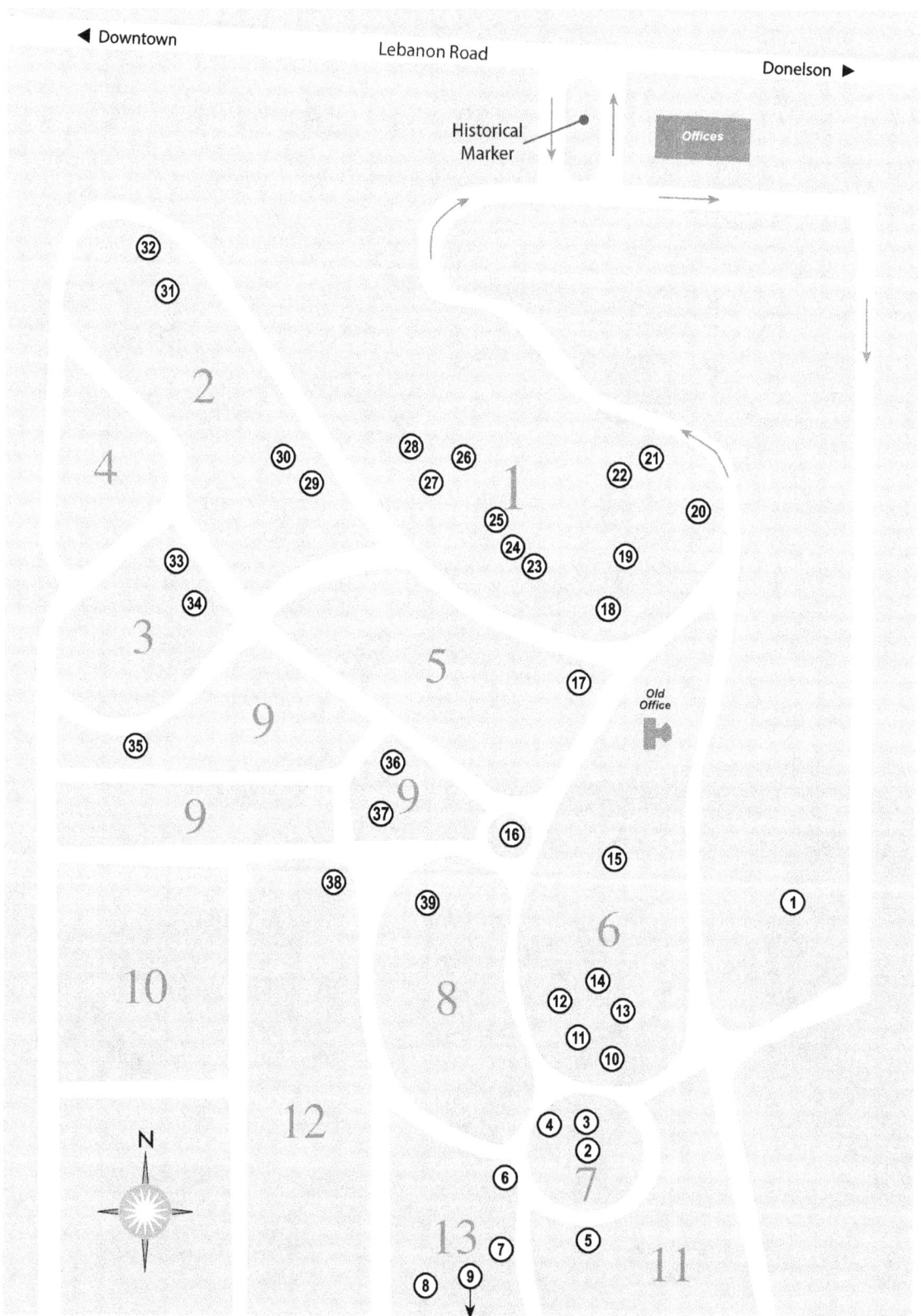

① **Confederate Memorial Hall**—Hillside holding crypt resembling a Gothic castle that has been converted into a self-guided museum containing interpretive panels of information and pictures about local Southern military heroes and personalities. Maintained by the Joseph Johnston Camp of the Sons of Confederate Veterans.

② **Confederate Circle**—Holds the graves of 1,500 soldiers in 13 rows encircling the 45-foot-tall granite monument of a Confederate infantryman. The first six rows are graves of Confederates from outside Tennessee; the seventh row is unknown soldiers; the outer rows are Tennesseans. The burial ground was dedicated in 1869 by the Ladies Memorial Society. The monument was unveiled May 16, 1889 with 10,000 persons present.

③ **Adolphus Heiman**—A native Prussian and master stonecutter who moved to America in 1834 and Nashville in 1836, Heiman (1809-1862) became one of Nashville's most esteemed architects. His Hospital for the Insane (1855) was one of the most inventive buildings in the U.S. Unfortunately many of his designs do not survive. A Mexican War hero, he commanded the Tennessee 10th Regiment of Irishmen during the Civil War. He was captured at Fort Donelson and died as a result of ill health contracted while a prisoner of war. First interred in Mississippi, his remains were moved here, beneath the monument, in 1869.

④ **Brigadier General Thomas Benton Smith**—One of the youngest generals, Benton Smith (1838-1923) was wounded at Stones River and in November 1864 was captured at Shy's Hill during the Battle of Nashville and assaulted by a Union colonel who struck him on the head with his sword. The exposed wound was thought to be fatal, but Smith survived until age 85, dying in 1923 after having spent most of his years after the war in an insane asylum.

⑤ **Acklen Family Mausoleum**—An impressive Gothic structure, the mausoleum holds the remains of Adelicia Acklen (1817-1887), mistress of Belmont Plantation, two of her three husbands, nine of her ten children, and one grandchild. The daughter of local pioneer Oliver B. Hayes, Adelicia married wealthy plantation owner Isaac Franklin in 1839 when she was 22 and he was 50. Franklin died in 1846, leaving her seven Louisiana cotton plantations, a Middle Tennessee farm, and 750 slaves. Fairvue, their estate, survives today as an affluent suburban community. She then married Col. Joseph Acklen, an astute businessman who tripled her holdings. They built Belmont, an opulent estate and summer home south of downtown Nashville. He died in 1863 during the Civil War; she subsequently played the Unionists against the Confederates and sold her cotton bales in England for nearly $1 million in gold. In 1867 at age 50 Mrs. Acklen married her third husband, Dr. William A. Cheatham. In 1886 she left him and Nashville, and moved to Washington, D.C. Dr. Cheatham is buried with his first wife in Section 14, Lot 240. Inside the Acklen mausoleum is Peri, a marble statue from Belmont Mansion's Grand Salon. The mausoleum was built in 1884, three years before Adelicia Acklen's death during a New York City shopping spree. Belmont Mansion, located on the Belmont University campus, is an antebellum house museum open to the public.

⑥ **Grundy Monument**—Known as Tennessee's greatest criminal lawyer, Felix Grundy (1777-1840) was a Virginian who first served in Kentucky, appointed Chief Justice in that state. He came to Nashville in 1807 and soon was elected to Congress, where he was a war hawk and supported President Madison in declaring war against Great Britain. He served in the U.S. Senate, 1829-38, and then as President Van Buren's Attorney General. He only served one year in that position before being re-appointed to the U.S. Senate. His wife, Ann Phillips Rogers of Kentucky, established the first Sunday School in Nashville. The couple was first buried at City Cemetery; their remains were moved here in 1890. A loyal and beloved slave, Ambrose, is also buried here.

⑦ **Brigadier General James E. Rains**—A descendant of a pioneer family, Rains (1833-1862) was educated at Yale, and served as an attorney, associate newspaper editor, city attorney, and district attorney before the Civil War. At Murfreesboro, on Dec. 31, 1862, he was killed instantly by a bullet leading his brigade against a Federal battery. His last words were, "Forward, my brave boys, forward!" He was first buried at City Cemetery, with the occupying Federal authorities allowing "no fuss" during the services. He was moved to Mount Olivet in 1888 with great ceremony.

⑧ **General William Hicks "Red" Jackson**—Jackson (1835-1903), a West Point graduate, fought at Holly Springs and in the Vicksburg Campaign, and commanded a division of cavalry under N.B. Forrest in late 1864. After the Civil War he married Selene Harding, daughter of General William Giles Harding, and managed Belle Meade Plantation for many years, making it the top-ranked thoroughbred horse farm in the South. He served as president of the Tennessee Bureau of Agriculture.

⑨ **Colonel David Campbell Kelley**—Kelley, the "Fighting Parson," served under General Nathan Bedford Forrest. In an unique engagement, Kelley's cavalrymen, armed with light artillery, fought off Union ironclad gunboats on six occasions on the Cumberland River from Dec. 2-15, 1864. The city greenway west of Nashville preserving the site is named Kelley's Battlefield. A Methodist minister, he was also instrumental in the founding of Vanderbilt University. His marker is in Section 15.

⑩ **Gentry Monument**—One of the finest orators in the U.S. Congress, Meredith Poindexter Gentry (1809-1866) was a Whig politician who later became a Confederate congressman.

⑪ **John Bell Monument**—A Nashville lawyer and state legislator, John Bell (1796-1869) served as Secretary of War, a U.S. Congressman, and as U.S. Senator before running for President on the Constitutional Union ticket in the 1860 election won by Abraham Lincoln. A slaveowner who argued against secession, he won the electoral votes of three states—Tennessee, Kentucky, and Virginia. Although he later sided with the South, he played no role in the hostilities.

⑫ **Cole Monument**—Colonel Edmund W. Cole (1827-1899) was president of the Nashville & Chattanooga Railroad from 1868-1880 and expanded the line west to the Mississippi River and east to the seaboard. He founded Nashville's American National Bank, and also

John Bell of Nashville served as Secretary of War and U.S. Senator before running for President in the 1860 election won by Abraham Lincoln. An anti-secessionist, Bell won the vote in Tennessee, Kentucky, and Virginia on the Constitutional Union Party ticket. Although he later sided with his native South, he played no part in the hostilities.

The Victorian Gothic vault bordering Confederate Circle holds the mortal remains of Adelicia Acklen, the mistress of the Belmont estate, along with two of her three husbands, nine of her ten children, and one grandchild. Adelicia Acklen was said to be the richest woman in America.

William B. Bate served as a Confederate general in the Civil War and as Tennessee Governor from 1882 to 1886.

Spinxes guard the pyramid crypt of Eugene C. Lewis (1845-1917), who served as the director general of the 1897 Tennessee Centennial Exposition. An arrow on the walkway in front of the pyramid points to true north.

the Randal Cole Industrial School in the memory of his deceased son. The school later became the Tennessee Industrial School. Another son served as chairman of the Board of Trust of Vanderbilt University. Their Southern Colonial mansion, Colemere, later served as a social club and a restaurant adjacent to the Nashville airport.

⑬ Gen. Alvan C. Gillem—A West Point graduate, General Alvan C. Gillem (1830-1875) was one of only six Tennesseans who served as Union generals during the war. He served as quartermaster under General George Thomas and Gen. Don C. Buell early in the war and then as Provost Marshal of Nashville. In June 1863 he was appointed adjutant general of Tennessee. His last action in 1873 was against Captain Jack and his Modoc followers who assassinated General Canby in northern California, driving them from the Lava Beds.

⑭ John W. Morton—Originally a member of the Rock City Guards (Nashville's pre-Civil War militia), Captain John W. Morton served ably as General N.B. Forrest's chief of artillery despite his young age (he celebrated his 21st birthday at the Battle of Chickamauga in 1863).

⑮ Bate Monument—General William Brimage Bate (1826-1905) was severely wounded at Shiloh, recovered, and went on to command at all battles of the Army of Tennessee from Dalton, Ga. to Greensboro, N.C. His division was overwhelmed on Shy's Hill at Nashville on Dec. 16, 1864. At various times in his life, he practiced law, fought in the Mexican War, edited a newspaper, and served in the General Assembly. As a "Bourbon Democrat," he served two terms as Governor, 1882-86. He served in the U.S. Senate from 1886 until his death.

⑯ Carter Mausoleum—The bright white Italian marble mausoleum with Moorish influences was built by Daniel F. Carter, wealthy banker and stagecoach owner, to house the remains of his son, John Carter, a Confederate soldier killed at the Battle of Perryville, Ky. in 1862. Also buried here is their daughter's husband, Thomas D. Craighead, grandson of the Rev. Thomas Craighead, the controversial Presbyterian pioneer preacher.

⑰ Anthony Van Leer Monument—Anthony Wayne Van Leer (1783-1863), a native of Chester County, Pa., was one of Tennessee's early industrialists, operating a highly profitable iron furnace at Cumberland Furnace, west of Nashville. He was the nephew of Revolutionary War General Anthony "Mad Anthony" Wayne. Van Leer's daughter, Eleanora, married Hugh Kirkman, son of a wealthy Nashville merchant. She died of childbirth in 1849. Van Leer Kirkman (1849-1911) served under Gen. Forrest during the Civil War. Eleanora and Hugh Kirkman's only daughter, Mary Florence (1843-1905), caused a stir when she married Union Army Captain James P. Drouillard of Ohio. Relatives refused to attend their wedding. The Drouillards moved to Cumberland Furnace after inheriting her grandfather's iron furnace. They built a grand Italianate mansion and held opulent parties there. By 1880, their furnace was producing 20 tons of pig iron a day and employed 250 workers. In 1886 they returned to Nashville and urban society.

⑱ General Gates P. Thruston Monument—General Gates P. Thruston (1835-1912) of the U.S. Army married Ida Hamilton, the daughter of prominent Nashvillians after the Civil War and became a business and civic leader. He later wrote the definitive book on Tennessee archaeology, *The Antiquities of Tennessee*, and donated his vast collection of artifacts and minerals to Vanderbilt University. The collection can be seen at the Tennessee State Museum. He was one of the reorganizers of the Tennessee Historical Society in 1875.

⑲ Major General Benjamin F. Cheatham—A descendant of one of the founding families of Nashville, General Cheatham (1820-1886) fought in every major Civil War battle of the Army of Tennessee. His men earned distinction during the Atlanta Campaign of 1864. Blamed by Gen. Hood for the escape of the Union army at Spring Hill in November 1864, his corps took the brunt of the horrific fighting at Franklin, Tenn. the next day. Two weeks later, his corps held the right flank on the first day of the Battle of Nashville, but lost the left flank the following day. He later became Superintendent of the state prison system and then Postmaster of Nashville. He was known as a plain speaker, hard drinker and hard fighter, and was beloved by his men.

⑳ Brigadier General William N.R. Beall—A native of Kentucky, Beall (1825-1883) was a West Point graduate who served in Arkansas under Confederate Gen. Van Dorn and later surrendered with his brigade at Port Hudson, La. in July 1863. He was imprisoned at Johnson Island, Ohio, and paroled to serve as an agent for the relief of Confederate prisoners in Northern prison camps. Stationed in New York City, he was allowed to sell cotton through the blockade and use the proceeds to purchase blankets and clothing for the POWs. After the war he became a merchant in St. Louis, Mo., and died in McMinnville, Tenn.

㉑ General George E. Maney—Born in Franklin, Tenn., Maney (1826-1901) was educated at the University of Nashville, fought in the Mexican War, and commanded the 1st Tennessee Regiment in the Civil War, fighting in battles from Shiloh to Atlanta. In 1868 he became president of the Tennessee & Pacific Railroad and he was the Republican nominee for governor in 1876. He occupied diplomatic posts in Colombia, Bolivia, Paraguay, and Uruguay. He died suddenly in Washington, D.C.

㉒ Harding/Jackson Monument—This plot contains 14 people, including John Harding (1777-1865), the founder of the famous Belle Meade estate, which was one of the nation's foremost thoroughbred horse farms (today a mansion/plantation museum open to the public), and wife Susannah Shute Harding; General William Giles Harding (1808-1886), who transformed the original 1820 house into a Greek Revival mansion in 1854 and who was imprisoned at Fort Mackinac, Mich. in 1862 due to his Confederate sympathies, and his two wives; their youngest daughter Mary and her husband, U.S. Senator and U.S. Supreme Court Justice Howell E. Jackson (1832-1895); and other family members.

㉓ Colonel Luke Lea—Descendant of pioneer families, Luke Lea (1879-1945) was a lawyer, crusader, ardent Prohibitionist, and publisher of the Nashville *Tennessean* (1907), which still exists. He raised the 114th Field Artillery Regiment, which fought in World War

In the southwest section of Mount Olivet Cemetery, in the corner of a large open field, is the white marble headstone of U.S. Private Oliver P. Rood of Company B of the 20th Indiana Volunteer Infantry Regiment (not listed on the map). He was 19 years old when he fought at the Battle of Gettysburg, in Pennsylvania, and on the second day of battle captured the Confederate battle flag of the 21st North Carolina Regiment of Hoke's Brigade. This brave action won him the Congressional Medal of Honor, as noted on the bronze marker at his grave. Pvt. Rood seems not to have married, and died on June 11, 1885 at the age of 41. There is no recorded reason why this Indiana native and Union hero of Gettysburg is buried in a Nashville cemetery noted as the final resting place for many prominent Confederate officers and enlisted men.

The "open" field in which he rests is actually the site of thousands of unmarked burials of the 19th Century.

The McGavock burial vault holds the remains of a distinguished family. Jacob McGavock (1790-1878) came to Nashville in 1807. He was an aide to General Andrew Jackson in the Creek Indian War. Later he served as U.S. Circuit Clerk. He and wife Louisa Caroline Grundy, daughter of Tennessee's finest criminal lawyer, raised 13 children. Randal McGavock (1826-1863) served as mayor in 1858 before leading the Tenth Tennessee Regiment to war. He was killed at Raymond, Miss., leading his regiment of Irishmen in battle. Jacob McGavock Dickinson (1851-1928) became an expert in international law and served as Secretary of War under President William Howard Taft and as successful U.S. Counsel in a 1903 dispute over the American-Canadian boundary of Alaska.

John Catron (1779-1865) was the first Tennessean to serve on the U.S. Supreme Court. He was appointed by President Andrew Jackson. Earlier he served as Chief Justice of the State Supreme Court. A Unionist, he left Nashville at the beginning of the Civil War and returned after the Federal occupation of the city in February 1862. The stone on the crypt is patterned to look like wood.

One. Following the armistice, Lea led a small band of soldiers into Holland in an unsuccessful bid to kidnap or persuade the German Kaiser to attend the Paris peace talks. After the war he advanced progressive causes and established a publishing empire, which failed during the Depression. He served two years in a North Carolina prison for banking violations but he later received a full pardon. In 1927, he donated the original 868 acres of Percy Warner Park to Nashville, requesting it be named in honor of his father-in-law.

(24) **Percy Warner**—A successful businessman, Percy Warner (1861-1927) ran the Nashville Railway and Light Co. and dabbled in public utilities across the state. His wife, Margaret Lindsley, was the daughter of noted educator Dr. John B. Lindsley. He served on the city's parks commission, and Nashville's largest park is now named for him. An avid bird collector at his Renraw estate, he was known to have a pet peacock which accompanied him everywhere.

(25) **Lindsley Monument**—Buried here are two distinguished Nashville educators, Dr. Philip Lindsley (1786-1855), the administrator of the University of Nashville (originally Cumberland College) for 25 years who had originally come from Princeton (N.J.) University, and his son, Dr. John Berrien Lindsley (1822-1897), a Presbyterian minister who established the Medical College and served as chancellor of the university, saving its buildings from destruction during the Civil War. He helped establish Montgomery Bell Academy and served as secretary to the State Board of Health.

(26) **John Overton Monument**—Judge John Overton (1766-1833), a Virginian, came to Nashville via Kentucky in 1789 and later built the Travellers Rest Plantation on the Franklin Pike (now a house/plantation museum open to the public). A lawyer and Superior Court judge, he became a close friend of Andrew Jackson. As a powerful political leader and banker he helped elect Jackson as President. He and Jackson and Sumner Countian Gen. James Winchester founded the city of Memphis on the Mississippi River in 1819.

(27) **Jacob McGavock Crypt**—Jacob McGavock (1790-1878) and wife Louisa Caroline Grundy (1798-1878), the daughter of Felix Grundy, had 13 children. McGavock came to Nashville in 1807 and served as an aide to Gen. Jackson during the Creek War. He also served as U.S. Circuit Court Clerk. His son, Colonel Randal McGavock (1826-1863), was educated at Harvard, served as mayor of Nashville, and commanded the 10th Tennessee "Irish" Regiment during the Civil War. He was killed at the Battle of Raymond, Miss., in May 1863. Jacob McGavock Dickinson (1851-1928) was a Confederate cavalryman, an expert in international law, president of the American Bar Association, and Secretary of War under President Taft. He helped settle the boundary between Canada and Alaska.

(28) **Catron Crypt**—John Catron (1786-1865) was the first Chief Justice of the Tennessee Supreme Court and the first Tennessean to serve on the U.S. Supreme Court, appointed by President Jackson in 1837. He was a Unionist during the Civil War, leaving Nashville until the Union Army captured and occupied it. His stone crypt was fashioned to resemble wood.

(29) **McAlister Monument**—Among family members here is Hill McAlister (1875-1959), who served as governor of Tennessee during the Great Depression. His great-grandfather Aaron Brown and great-great-grandfather Willie Blount were also governors. His wife, Louise Jackson McAlister (1879-1955) was daughter of Supreme Court Justice Howell Jackson. Hill McAlister's parents are also buried here; his father, Judge William King McAlister (1850-1923) served on the Tennessee Supreme Court.

(30) **Aaron V. Brown Monument**—Aaron V. Brown (1795-1859) was a native Virginian who came to Nashville to practice law. He served in both houses of Tennessee and in the U.S. House of Representatives. He was elected Governor in 1845-47 and issued the call for 2,600 men to serve in the Mexican War. Thirty thousand responded, reinforcing Tennessee's reputation as the "Volunteer State." He served as Postmaster General under President Buchanan. His second wife was the sister of General Gideon Pillow.

(31) **Oliver B. Hayes Monument**—Oliver B. Hayes (1783-1858) was an early settler who came to Nashville in 1808 to practice law. He was a law partner with Thomas Hart Benton. He resided at the Rokeby mansion and later became a Presbyterian minister. He is probably best known as the father of Adelicia Acklen.

(32) **Eugene C. Lewis Crypt**—Eugene C. Lewis (1845-1917) was the chief engineer of the Nashville, Chattanooga and St. Louis Railroad and director general of the Tennessee Centennial Exposition in 1897. He suggested the building of a replica of the Greek Parthenon for the expo, now perhaps Nashville's defining landmark. Lewis also was instrumental in the building of Union Station at the turn of the century; the structure is now a luxury hotel. A member of the Memphis Order of Masons, his crypt is a pyramid guarded by two sphinxes. The arrow embedded in the walkway points to true north.

(33) **Robert B.C. Howell Monument**—Robert Boyte Crawford Howell (1801-1868) served as pastor of the First Baptist Church, first editor of *The Tennessee Baptist*, and president of the Southern Baptist Convention. His son, Morton Boyte Howell, was Mayor of Nashville in 1874-75 and president of the Mt. Olivet Cemetery Co. from 1898-1909.

(34) **Samuel Watkins Monument**—When brick manufacturer, businessman, and the wealthiest man in Nashville Samuel Watkins died in 1880 he bequeathed $100,000 and property to start a free school for youths who lived in poverty, just as he once did in his native Virginia. This institution also became instrumental in teaching new immigrants and later as a center for adult education. Today, it survives as Watkins Institute of Art and Design. Before his death, Watkins also served as bank director and president of the gas-light company, streetcar company, and city Board of Education.

(35) **Furman Monument**—Mary J. Furman had this impressive monument (the largest in the cemetery) built for her husband, wealthy merchant Francis Furman (1816-1899) and also bequeathed money for a building in his name at Vanderbilt University. The monument (photo on page 20) is patterned after the Porch of Maidens at the Erechtheum in Athens, Greece. The statues of maidens are called caryatids; each one is different from the rest. The Furman monument

The black granite monument of Vernon King Stevenson, the "Father of Tennessee Railroads," is an exact copy of Napoleon Bonaparte's tomb in Paris. The city of Stevenson, Ala. is named for him.

The Warner Monument mourns three young children who died of cholera.

A beautiful Celtic cross marks the gravesite of Anne Dallas Dudley (1876-1955) who was a major force in the temperance movement and the women's suffrage movement, resulting in the ratification of the Nineteenth Amendment in 1920. She helped organize the Women's Civic League in Nashville. Her husband was Guilford Dudley, a founder of the Life and Casualty Insurance Company. Dallas, Texas, is named after her great-grandfather's brother, George M. Dallas.

A steamboat graces the gravestone of Captain Thomas Ryman (1841-1904) whose river packets hauled cargo along a 700-mile route from Kentucky to Indiana. In 1885 Ryman was converted to Christianity by the Rev. Sam Jones at a tent revival. Ryman then built the Union Gospel Tabernacle downtown. From his new house atop Rutledge Hill, Ryman could watch his riverboats and the tabernacle. After his death in 1904, the huge tabernacle was renamed the Ryman Auditorium, now a National Historic Landmark.

measures 22 feet by 12 feet and stands 18 feet tall.

㊱ Thomas Ryman Monument—The monument of riverboat captain Thomas Green Ryman (1841-1904) features an image of a steamboat and a fishing skiff. Ryman was a rough and tumble riverman along the Cumberland until he was converted to Christianity by the Rev. Sam Jones at a tent revival. Ryman built the Union Gospel Tabernacle for Jones to use in his revivals. The barn-like venue went on to host the nation's prominent entertainers and celebrities. It was renamed the Ryman Auditorium upon Ryman's death. In the 1940s it became home to the Grand Ole Opry and is known as the Mother Church of Country Music. Once slated to be torn down, the Ryman was saved and restored, and today hosts numerous musical events.

㊲ Warner Monument—The three childlike figures gathered around the Christ figure represent the three children of Leslie and Katharine Burch Warner, all of whom died of cholera within a year's time in the 1880s. Leslie Warner was the son of James C. Warner, an early iron manufacturer. His wife was the daughter of John C. Burch, editor of the *Nashville American* newspaper and secretary of the U.S. Senate. The couple retired early and traveled England and Europe. Leslie Warner died in 1909. Kate Warner became one of the most influential suffragists, working tirelessly for the right of women to vote. She was the first president of the Tennessee Women Suffrage Association. Tennessee was the deciding state in ratifying the Nineteenth Amendment in 1920.

The old cemetery office and chapel was built in 1872 in the American Gothic Revival style by Hugh Cathcart Thompson, a prominent finish carpenter and by the 1880s one of Nashville's premier builders of fine homes and churches. The office featured an octagonal vestry and an ornate belfry. This structure no longer stands.

㊳ Dallas Celtic Cross—Anne Dallas Dudley (1876-1955), wife of Guilford Dudley, a founder of the Life & Casualty Insurance Co., was a leader in the fight for women's suffrage and instrumental in Tennessee's ratification of the 19th Amendment in 1920. She served as president of the Tennessee Equal Suffrage Association and helped organize the Woman's Civic League of Nashville. Her grandfather, Commodore Alexander James Dallas, fired the first shot of the War of 1812; her great-grandfather, Alexander James Dallas, was President Madison's Secretary of the Treasury, and his brother, George M. Dallas, was U.S. Vice-President under James Polk. The city of Dallas, Texas, is named for him.

㊴ Stevenson Crypt—The black granite tomb of Vernon King Stevenson (1812-1884), the "Father of Tennessee Railroads," is an exact copy of Napoleon Bonaparte's tomb in Paris. He was a railroading pioneer and president of the Nashville and Chattanooga Railroad. The city of Stevenson, Ala. is named for him. He was criticized for abandoning his post as Confederate quartermaster in Nashville as the Union Army invaded Tennessee and captured Nashville with its vast warehouse stores. Later he secretly sold his shares in the locally owned Nashville & Chattanooga Railroad to the Louisville & Nashville Railroad. At his death, his estate was valued at $5 million, a vast sum at that time.

Limestone statues and other elaborate monuments to the dead are prevalent in Victorian cemeteries such as Mount Olivet.

Mount Olivet Cemetery
Notable Burials Not Marked on the Walking Tour Map

Other notables at Mount Olivet Cemetery whose gravesites are not located within the area covered by the walking tour map:

Knowles Fred Rose (1897-1954) was a founder of Music City USA, launching Nashville's first country music publishing house, Acuff-Rose Publications, with Roy Acuff in 1942. One of their first clients was Hank Williams. Rose was a gifted editor and talent scout. He got his start in Chicago as a pop songwriter and radio performer. From 1938-1942 he wrote songs for Gene Autry movies in Hollywood. He was elected to the Country Music Hall of Fame in 1961. (Section 27).

Stoneman Family. Ernest Van "Pop" Stoneman (1893-1968), a Virginia native, was the patriarch of a singing family which won the CMA's Vocal Group of the Year in 1967. In 2008 Stoneman was inducted into the Country Music Hall of Fame. During the 1920s he recorded more than 200 songs and participated in the historic Bristol Sessions in 1927 which led to the discoveries of The Carter Family and Jimmie Rodgers. Other members buried here are his wife Harriet F. "Hattie" Stoneman (1900-1976), Calvin S. "Scotty" Stoneman (1932-1973), Oscar J. "Jimmy" Stoneman (1937-2002), and Van Haden Stoneman (1940-1995).

Cornelia Clark Fort (1919-1943) was a Nashville debutante who learned how to fly and became a flight instructor. She was giving a flying lesson in Hawaii on Dec. 7, 1941 when the Japanese attacked Pearl Harbor. During the war she became a member of the Women's Air Force Service Pilots (WASPs), flying new aircraft from the factories to the air bases. On a ferrying mission in 1943 from Long Beach, Calif. to Dallas, Texas, she was killed in a mid-air collision. Her gravestone reads: "Killed in the Service of Her Country." A general aviation airport in East Nashville was named for her. (Section 25).

Tolbert Fanning (1810-1874) was an early leader of the Stone-Campbell religious movement in the South. He edited and published religious journals. A proponent of scientific agriculture, he helped found the State Agricultural Society and introduced the Morgan horse into Tennessee. He founded Franklin College on his farm where the present-day Nashville Airport is located. (Section 25).

David Lipscomb (1831-1917) was a student of Franklin College and Tolbert Fanning, a leader of the Disciples of Christ, and later the Churches of Christ, longtime editor of the *Gospel Advocate*, and co-founder in 1891 of the Nashville Bible School, which is now Lipscomb University. (Section 26).

Horace Greeley "H.G." Hill (1873-1942) was the founder of the H.G. Hill Grocery store chain, which at one time operated 500 stores in the South. He was a pioneer in self-service, cash and carry, and newspaper advertising. The H.G. Hill Realty Co. was one of the major real estate firms in Tennessee. He was also known as a public philanthropist. (Section 21).

Edwin Warner (1870-1945), who served as a Metro Parks commissioner, was one of the founders of Nashville's Percy Warner and Edwin Warner Parks in southwest Davidson County, the largest public parks in Tennessee. (Section 26).

The monument to **1st Lt. James A. Pigue** (1884-1918), who was killed in action in Belgium and remains buried there, features a life-size statue of the uniformed soldier standing at attention, and tributes to his mother and fraternal grandmother. (Section 25).

CONFEDERATE CIRCLE

at Mount Olivet Cemetery is the final resting place of 1,500 Confederate soldiers. Anchoring the circle is a 45-foot-tall granite monument topped by a nine-foot-tall statue of a Confederate soldier. The first six rows of graves encircling the monument are of soldiers from outside Tennessee; the seventh row is unknown soldiers; and the outer six rows are Tennesseans. The plot was purchased in 1869; the monument dedicated in 1889. In or near the circle are the burial sites of seven Confederate generals—William B. Bate, William N.R. Beall, Benjamin F. Cheatham, William H. Jackson, George E. Maney, James E. Rains, and Thomas Benton Smith. Also nearby are the graves of Col. Adolphus Heiman, Col. Randal McGavock, Col. David C. Kelley, and Capt. John W. Morton. Modern signage interprets the lives of many of those buried here.

Calvary Catholic Cemetery

Calvary Catholic Cemetery, owned by the Roman Catholic Diocese of Nashville, is located at 1001 Lebanon Pike, adjacent to Mt. Olivet Cemetery. The phone is (615) 256-4590.

Calvary Cemetery was dedicated on Nov. 29, 1868. Patrick A. Freehan, third Catholic Bishop of Tennessee, preached to a crowd of 4,000 people. The 47 acres of the cemetery were purchased for $15,000, "a great bargain." Many burials at the old City Cemetery were reinterred at Calvary, especially after the railroad tracks cut off Catholic burial sites from the main cemetery tract.

The procession leading to the dedication ceremony consisted of a band and 20 "neatly uniformed policemen," the bishop's carriage with four accompanying priests, and carriages containing members of the St. Vincent de Paul Society, the Society of St. Mary's Orphan Asylum, the St. Joseph's Abstinence Society, the school children from the Sisters of Mercy School, and carriages containing citizens.

Top Left: Calvary Cemetery is adorned with statuary, crypts, obelisks, and other monuments.

Left: The neatly organized gravesites of Catholic nuns at Calvary are marked by simple stone crosses enscribed with "Requiescat in Pace," Latin for Rest in Peace.

Above Right: The Bishops' Circle is adorned with the Crucifixion scene and ringed by the gravesites of Catholic priests.

Right: A cherub is carved on one of the many gravestones of Catholic citizens of Nashville born in Ireland.

Mount Ararat Cemetery (Greenwood West)

Mount Ararat Cemetery (1869) on Elm Hill Pike near Fesslers Lane is the oldest existing burial site for African-Americans in Nashville. Black businessman Nelson Walker created the site by buying property from John Trimble in the Cameron-Trimble Bottom. Because of periodic epidemics in Nashville, 1,400 burials per year took place at the cemetery. After years of neglect, the cemetery was assumed in 1982 by the Greenwood Cemetery Board and in 1986 its name was changed to Greenwood Cemetery West. Among others buried here is Dr. Robert Fulton Boyd, a black physician and graduate of Meharry Medical College who ran for mayor and helped found the National Medical Association, a national association for black physicians.

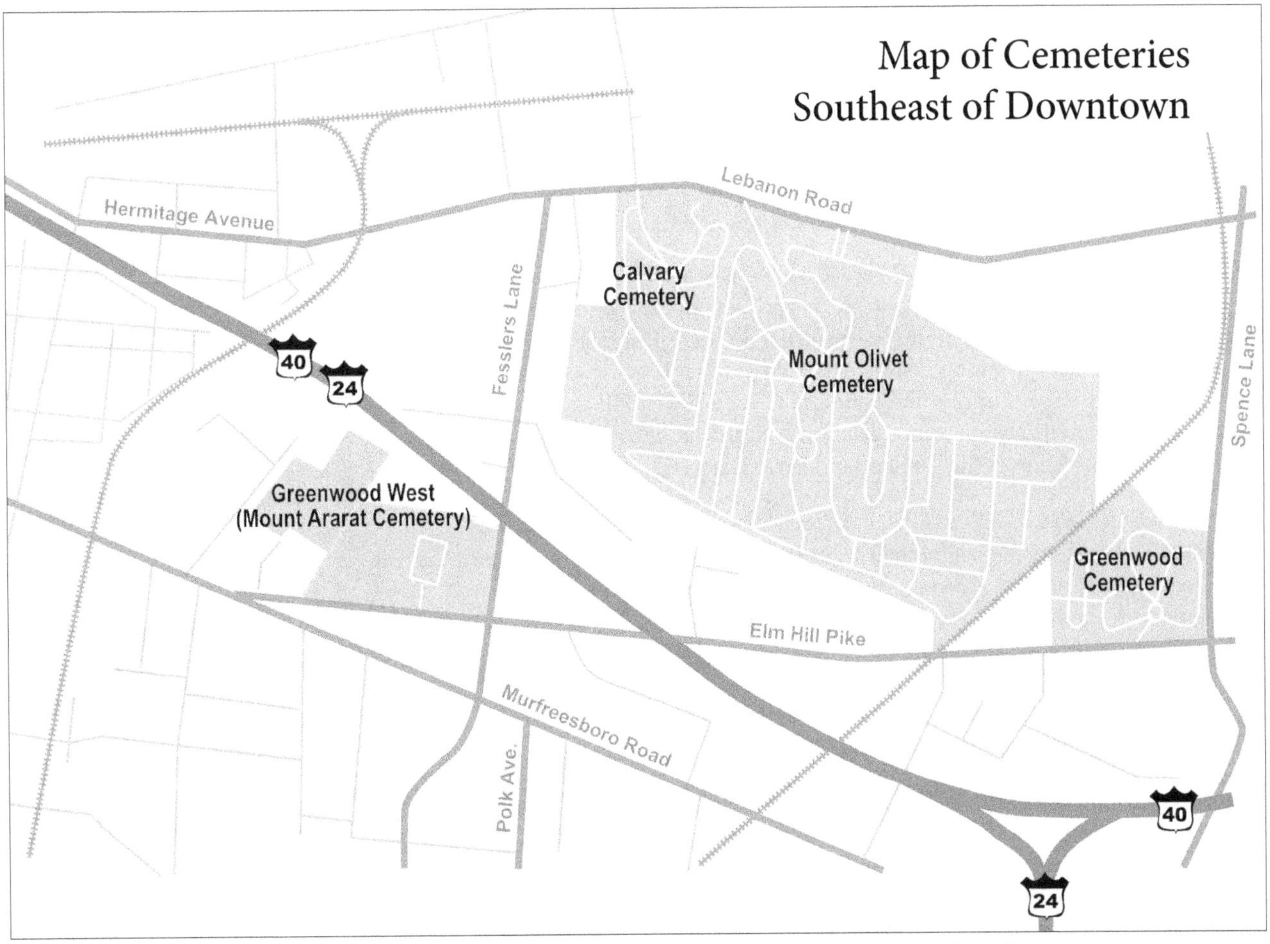

Map of Cemeteries Southeast of Downtown

TRAVEL NOTE: There is no direct motorway from Calvary Cemetery to Mount Olivet Cemetery or from Mount Olivet Cemetery to Greenwood Cemetery.

Greenwood Cemetery

Greenwood Cemetery at Elm Hill Pike and Spence Lane was founded in 1888 by **Preston Taylor**, minister and founder of the Lea Avenue Christian Church, founder of Greenwood Park, and one of the founders of Citizens Bank. Taylor was also an undertaker who opened the first black undertaking business in Nashville and operated a casket factory. The cemetery office phone is (615) 256-4395.

Outstanding Nashvillians buried in Greenwood Cemetery include Taylor and his wife; three original **Fisk Jubilee Singers**; **Deford Bailey**, the first black Grand Ole Opry performer; Tennessee State University Coach **John A. Merritt**; Nashville businessman **Richard H. Boyd** and son **Henry A. Boyd**; and civil rights leader **Kelly Miller Smith Sr.** and NFL quarterback **Joe Gilliam Jr.**

Preston Taylor (1849-1931) was born of slave parents in Louisiana and served as a drummer boy in the Union army. He moved to Nashville in 1884. He served as minister of the Gay Street Christian Church. He organized the 1917 National Colored Christian Missionary Convention and helped create the Tennessee State Agricultural and Industrial School. He married Georgia Gordon, one of the original Fisk Jubilee Singers. She died in 1913, and he married Ida D. Mallory. In 1906, Taylor established Greenwood Park adjacent to Greenwood Cemetery. The privately owned park opened at a time when African-American citizens were not permitted in public parks. Encompassing almost 40 acres of open land, Greenwood Park included a clubhouse, theater, skating rink, roller coaster, shooting gallery, merry-go-round, and baseball park (home of the Greenwood Giants). The annual State Colored Fair was conducted there. Today the site of the park is noted by a historical marker.

Kelly Miller Smith Sr. (1920-1984) served as the pastor of the First Baptist Church on Capitol Hill from 1951 to 1984. As president of the Nashville Christian Leadership Conference, he helped organize in 1960 the famous sit-ins which led to the desegregation of Nashville's downtown lunch counters. He also served as Assistant Dean of the Vanderbilt Divinity School, president of the Nashville NAACP, and as a founder of the Nashville Urban League. The Jefferson Street bridge over the Cumberland River is named in his memory.

John A. Merritt (1926-1983) was the highly successful head coach of the Tennessee State University Tigers football team from 1963 to 1983, compiling a record of 172-33-7 over 20 winning seasons. He was Coach of the Year in 1973. His teams won six national championships and four black college football titles, and had four undefeated seasons. Among the 23 TSU players who went to the NFL were Ed "Too Tall" Jones and Joe Gilliam. Prior to TSU, Big John Merritt coached at Versailles (Ky.) High School and Jackson State University. John A. Merritt Boulevard near TSU is named for him.

Joseph W. Gilliam Jr. (1950-2000) played quarterback for John Merritt at TSU and won championships in 1970 and 1971. Known as "Jefferson Street Joe," he was drafted by the Pittsburgh Steelers and became one of the first African-American quarterbacks to start an NFL game. His stardom was short-lived and he fell victim to drug abuse. He died at age 49. Six hundred people attended his funeral. His father, Joe Gilliam Sr., was the defensive coordinator at TSU under Merritt.

The monument to community activist and businessman Preston Taylor.

William B. Reed (1849-1934), known as Uncle Billy, worked for the Nashville, Chattanooga & St. Louis Railroad. His creed was to "love My Lord, My Home, and My Job."

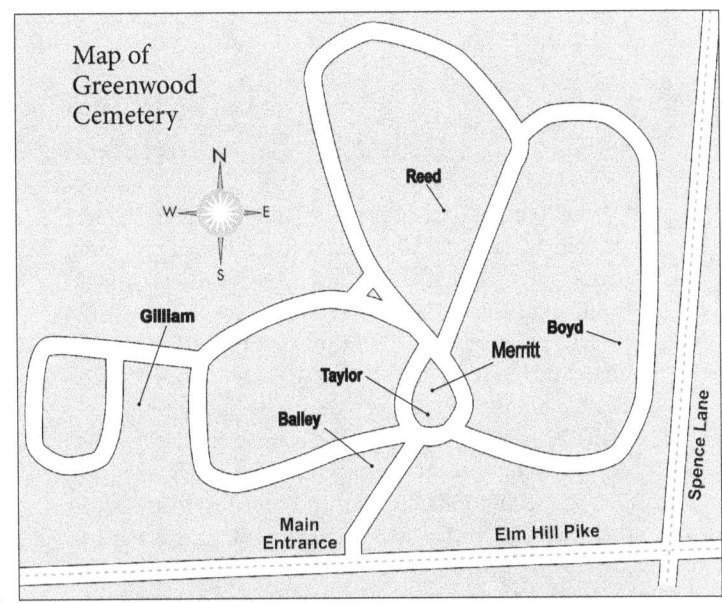

Deford Bailey (1899-1982) was striken with polio at age three growing up in rural Smith County, Tenn., and learned to play the harmonica. The disease stunted his growth but not his ambition. After moving to Nashville in 1918 his harmonica playing was discovered, and by 1928 he was appearing on the *Grand Ole Opry* more than any other performer. In 1928 he participated in the first Nashville recording session. He left the Opry in 1941 and retired from performing, returning in the 1970s to do a series of guest performances on the Opry. He is best known for his rendition of "Pan American Blues," making his harmonica sound like a train.

Richard Henry Boyd (1855-1922) was born a slave in Mississippi, and given the name Dick Gray by his master. After the Civil War, he moved to Texas, changed his name, and trained for the ministry. He moved to Nashville in 1896 and established the National Baptist Publishing Board, a religious publishing house. It became the largest black-owned publishing business in the U.S. Still in family hands, the NBPB prints more than 14 million books and periodicals a year. Boyd also co-founded the One-Cent Savings Bank, now Citizens Bank.

Boyd's son, **Henry Allen Boyd** (1876-1959) co-founded the *Nashville Globe,* a prominent newspaper in Nashville's African-American community until 1960. He was a strong advocate of the black-owned business community. After his father's death, he continued the successful operation of the NBPB publishing house. He was instrumental in having the Tennessee Agricultural and Industrial State Normal College for Negroes (Tennessee State University) located in Nashville.

The Reverend Richard Henry Boyd (1855-1922) was the founder of the National Baptist Publishing Board and one of the founders of Citizens Bank. A civil rights leader, he helped lead the 1905 Nashville streetcar boycott.

The gravesite of Joe Gilliam, Jr., who played pro football for Tennessee State University and the Pittsburgh Steelers.

Temple Jewish Cemetery
First Jewish Cemetery in Nashville, Dating to 1851

The Temple Jewish Cemetery at 2001 15th Avenue North dates to 1851 when five families and eight young men, Nashville's earliest Jewish settlers, bought three acres in north Nashville to create the city's first Jewish cemetery. Today the cemetery is nine acres, contains 3,000 burials, and serves the Temple Congregation Ohabai Sholom, the city's oldest. The phone number is (615) 255-9077. Nearby are the cemeteries for the West End Synagogue and Congregation Sherith Israel.

At the time of its creation the cemetery was "out in the country." Today it is a rare patch of greenery in the midst of urban congestion. It has recently benefitted from a three-year restoration program. In 2004 the cemetery was added to the National Register of Historic Places.

In the Jewish tradition there are few flowers placed at the cemetery; the custom is to leave a stone on the grave.

In 1886 a brick arched gate flanked by towers was built along with a domed chapel. These exuberant Victorian structures were demolished in 1966.

Among those buried at Temple Cemetery is Zadoc Levy, a German tailor who in 1855 opened a clothing store, now operating as Levy's clothing store in Green Hills. One of the few sculptures is at the tomb of Felix Salzkotter, a child of eleven who died in 1872.

The Benjamin Herman family rests in a classical temple mausoleum (1899). The family sold wholesale dry goods, boots, and shoes. The Kornman-Raskin vault of 1918 is Egyptian Revival with an emblem of Amon Ra, the sun god, in the cavetto cornice over the door.

Judah Bloomstein, once one of the city's wealthiest Jews, was imprisoned in 1863 during the Civil War for smuggling supplies to the Confederates. Dr. Jacob Mitchell was one of the cemetery's three original founders. He rejected traditional medicine in favor of the roots and herbs used by Native Americans.

The following text can be found on the cemetery website:

"A cemetery in Hebrew is called a Beit Hayyim, a house of the living, and tours conducted in the cemetery introduce visitors to the history of the Nashville Jewish community through the individuals buried there. Because the non-Jewish wife of one of the original purchasers of the property had converted to Judaism in her native Holland, where no one was permitted to change their religion, upon her death in 1856, special rabbinic permission had to be granted for her interment in the cemetery. An officer in the Union Army, Lt. Julius Lettman, was buried at the cemetery after being killed in the Battle of Murfreesboro in 1863. S.A. Bierfield was killed by the Ku Klux Klan in nearby Franklin, Tenn. in 1868. In 1866, Joseph Lowenheim narrowly escaped death at the hands of Klansmen when he was able to make a Masonic sign, which one of his attackers recognized."

Mill Creek Baptist Church Cemetery
One of the Oldest Cemeteries in Davidson County

The tall monument to George and Sarah Ridley testifies that they were "Enemies to vice and unacquainted with hypocrisy, plain in their manner of life but always affable and kind, they added the pure religion of the bible to their many earthly blessings and looked upon the grave as the last stepping stone to another and a better world." George died in 1835 at the age of 98 and Sarah died the next year at age 81.

Samuel Ham died October 23, 1854 at the age of 79. A native of Amherst County, Va., he moved to Tennessee "and settled near this spot in 1794, where he spent the remainder of his days."

At the corner of Old Glenrose Avenue and Dodge Drive, tucked between the railroad tracks and noisy Interstate 24, is the old Mill Creek Baptist Church graveyard, one of the oldest cemeteries in Davidson County. The cemetery grew around the Mill Creek Baptist Church, organized in 1795 by the Menees and Whitsitt families. A log structure was built in 1797, to be replaced in 1810 by a brick meeting house. Nothing remains of the old church.

Churches arising from Mill Creek's missions include Antioch, First Church, Nashville, Grandview, Concord, Rock Springs, and Providence. The State Baptist Convention was organized at Mill Creek in 1833.

The graveyard contains 150 known and several unknown graves of early settlers, pioneers, and slaves. Working to preserve the graveyard is the Friends of Mill Creek Baptist Church Graveyard.

NASHVILLE NATIONAL CEMETERY

The Nashville National Cemetery is located at 1420 Gallatin Road in Madison, just north of the Briley Parkway interchange. The national cemetery covers 64.5 acres and contains 34,823 interments as of 2006. The phone is (615) 860-0086. Visitation is daily from dawn to dusk. Office hours are Monday-Friday, 7:30 to 5.

This hallowed ground was established as a U.S. Military Cemetery on Jan. 28, 1867. Originally there were 16,489 burials of known Union soldiers and employees: 38 officers, 10,300 white soldiers, 1,447 colored soldiers, and 703 employees. Among the unknown, there were 3,098 white soldiers, 463 colored soldiers, and 29 employees.

The location north of downtown was chosen by U.S. General George Thomas. He chose a site alongside the Louisville & Nashville Railroad tracks because he wanted everyone arriving from the north to see the sacrifices made during the war. At one time a special platform was built to serve as a train stop.

The Union deceased were gathered from an extensive region of Middle Tennessee and southern Kentucky. The number of distinct burial places from which these bodies were taken was 251. A large proportion of the dead, however, were transferred from the hospital burial grounds in and around Nashville and from the nearby battlefields of Franklin and Gallatin, Tenn. Reinterments were also made from Bowling Green and Cave City, Ky.

Minnesota's Troops

Why does the Nashville National Cemetery feature a monument to the State of Minnesota? During the Civil War, Minnesota, a state for only three years, sent only eleven regiments to fight. The regiments, despite also having to fight back home in the Dakota Indian War of 1862-63, served all over the country and earned hard-fought fame. Minnesota monuments can be found at Gettysburg, Shiloh, Vicksburg, Chickamauga, and Chattanooga.

The Fifth, Seventh, Ninth, and Tenth Regiments, along with the Second Minnesota Light Artillery, served at the Battle of Nashville on Dec. 15-16, 1864 and suffered more than 300 casualties, ten percent of the Union total. Many of those men are buried at Nashville, which was the single deadliest battle for Minnesotans during the war.

Also at the time, the 8th Minnesota was posted at nearby Murfreesboro and lost 90 men in a sharp confrontation Dec. 7th with Gen. N.B. Forrest's troopers. In addition, the 11th Minnesota regiment was pulling garrison duty at nearby Gallatin, Tenn.

The Nashville regiments were part of General A.J. Smith's rugged "guerillas," who arrived by steamboat on December 1st after marching and campaigning for hundreds of miles in Missouri.

On the first day of battle, the 7th Minnesota and 10th Minnesota helped overwhelm and capture Confederate redoubts five and three, respectively, but the fiercest fighting came on the afternoon of December 16th, as General John McArthur's division stormed up Shy's Hill, the left flank of the Confederate line.

At about 3 o'clock the buglers signaled the start of a barrage by 18 Union cannons. Ordered by McArthur to "take that hill," the lead brigade marched off at the double-quick with drawn bayonets and assaulted the steep hill. The 10th Minnesota on the left wing took the brunt of casualties, losing 70 men, including eight of 23 officers, to flanking fire. "A perfect storm of musket balls rained continuously upon us," stammered one soldier. The regimental commander, Lt. Col. Samuel Jennison, was severely wounded.

Battle of Nashville at Shy's Hill by Howard Pyle. Painting hangs in Minnesota State Capitol.

Colonel Lucius F. Hubbard commanded the Second Brigade, led by the 5th Minnesota and 9th Minnesota. The men marched 600 yards across a soggy cornfield, wracked by enfilading canister fire at 400 yards away. Hubbard had two horses shot from under him and was knocked down by a minie ball in the neck. He managed to get back up and keep charging. The entire brigade suffered about 300 casualties out of 1,421 men. The 5th Minnesota suffered a third of those casualties, including four flag-bearers. Thomas Gere of the 5th captured the battle flag of the 4th Mississippi Regiment and received the Congressional Medal of Honor. "The fighting was the heaviest in our front—it was indeed a desperate thing to go through that storm of grape, canister, and musket balls—we who got through wonder how we escaped," he later wrote.

Colonel William R. Marshall of the 7th Minnesota led the Third Brigade, which managed to fall upon the Confederates in their sector with some surprise, driving skirmishers before them so that the Confederate regulars could not fire lest they hit their own men. Marshall later served as governor of Minnesota.

The desperate assault upon Shy's Hill—ending in vicious hand-to-hand fighting—was wildly successful and decisive. With the Confederate left flank broken, the entire Confederate line quickly retreated south to the Brentwood Hills in varying degrees of order. Captured were 1,533 Confederate soldiers, 85 officers, four battle flags, and eight cannon. The Minnesotans engaged at Shy's Hill argued for decades which regiment had been first to the summit and which had captured the most prisoners.

Nashville National Cemetery Tour Map

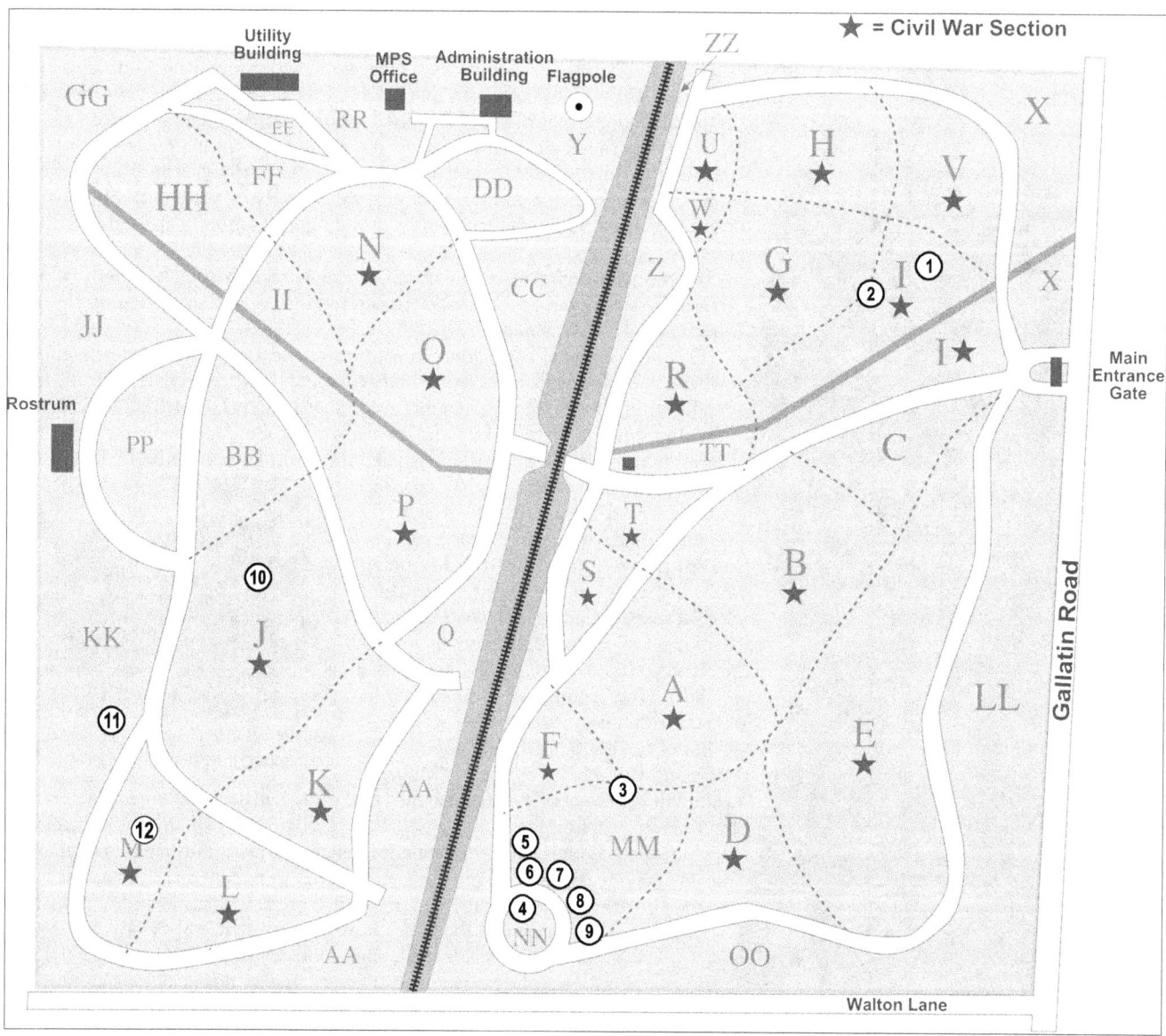

Nashville National Cemetery

① Medal of Honor Recipient **Private Charles Cantrell** (grave marker Sec. I, No. 132).

② Medal of Honor Recipient **Corporal William Lyell** (grave marker Sec. I, No. 151).

③ **Minnesota State Monument** (1920). Minnesota lost more soldiers at the Battle of Nashville, Dec. 15-16, 1864, than in any other single combat engagement in American history. Minnesota, which had only been a state for three years and was fighting the Dakota Indian War, sent only 11 regiments south to fight in the Civil War. Many of those lost were involved in the decisive attack Dec. 16th at Shy's Hill.

A common marker at Nashville's National Cemetery—a U.S. soldier killed during the Civil War whose identity is known only to God. There are thousands of such burials in the cemetery.

④ **Staff Sergeant Barry A. Sadler** (1940-1989) served in Vietnam and wrote the famous song, "The Ballad of the Green Beret." The song was the biggest hit single of 1966. He also wrote several books. In 1989 he was shot in the head under mysterious circumstances while riding in a taxi-cab in Guatemala City. He was brought to the U.S. and remained in a coma for several months. He died at his mother's home in Murfreesboro, Tenn. He is buried in Section NN, No. 64.

⑤ **Herman Bader** (d.1899), Captain, Co. F of the 29th Missouri Regiment. Commander of the Grand Army of the Republic George H. Thomas Post, No. 1 Dept. of Tennessee. General Thomas led the Federals at the Battle of Nashville in 1864. He also chose the site for the Nashville National Cemetery.

⑥ **Col. Edward S. Jones** (1813-1886), Commander, 3rd Pennsylvania Cavalry. Founder and commander of the Tennessee-Georgia Department of the Grand Army of the Republic.

⑦ **Col. James W. Lawless** (1832-1899), 5th Kentucky Cavalry. A native of Ireland, he came to the U.S. at the age of 16.

⑧ **Chaplain Erastus M. Cravath** (1833-1900), 101st Ohio Volunteer Infantry Regiment. He was one of the founders of historically black Fisk University in Nashville and served as its president for 25 years.

⑨ **West Patterson** (1831-1905), 4th Pennsylvania Volunteer Cavalry. "Teacher of freedmen for 31 years" reads his headstone.

⑩ Statue of **U.S. Colored Troops** infantryman, dedicated in 2006.

⑪ Medal of Honor Recipient **Corporal John Carr** (grave marker Sec. KK, No. 16550).

⑫ **James A. Leonard** (1813-1864), 1st Kansas Battery. His unique marker, a short spire, is one of oldest in the cemetery. He was killed by guerillas in January 1864 (grave marker 16234).

Recipients of the Congressional Medal of Honor

Corporal William F. Lyell

Rank and organization: Corporal, U.S. Army, Company F, 17th Infantry Regiment, 7th Infantry Division. Place and date: Near Chup'a-ri, Korea, 31 August 1951. Entered service at: Old Hickory, Tenn. Birth: Hickman County, Tenn. G.O. No.: 4, 9 January 1953.

Citation:

Cpl. Lyell, a member of Company F, distinguished himself by conspicuous gallantry and outstanding courage above and beyond the call of duty in action against the enemy. When his platoon leader was killed, Cpl. Lyell assumed command and led his unit in an assault on strongly fortified enemy positions located on commanding terrain. When his platoon came under vicious, raking fire which halted the forward movement, Cpl. Lyell seized a 57mm recoilless rifle and unhesitatingly moved ahead to a suitable firing position from which he delivered deadly accurate fire completely destroying an enemy bunker, killing its occupants. He then returned to his platoon and was resuming the assault when the unit was again subjected to intense hostile fire from two other bunkers. Disregarding his personal safety, armed with grenades he charged forward hurling grenades into one of the enemy emplacements, and although painfully wounded in this action he pressed on destroying the bunker and killing six of the foe. He then continued his attack against a third enemy position, throwing grenades as he ran forward, annihilating four enemy soldiers. He then led his platoon to the north slope of the hill where positions were occupied from which effective fire was delivered against the enemy in support of friendly troops moving up. Fearlessly exposing himself to enemy fire, he continuously moved about directing and encouraging his men until he was mortally wounded by enemy mortar fire. Cpl. Lyell's extraordinary heroism, indomitable courage, and aggressive leadership reflect great credit on himself and are in keeping with the highest traditions of the military service.

Private Charles Cantrell

Rank and Organization: Private, Company F, 10th U.S. Infantry.
Place and Date: At Santiago, Cuba, 1 July 1898.
Entered Service At: Nashville, Tenn.
Born: 13 February 1874, Smithville, Tenn.
Date of Issue: 22 June 1899.
Citation: Gallantly assisted in the rescue of the wounded from in front of the lines and under heavy fire from the enemy.

Corporal John Carr

Rank and organization: Private, Company G, 8th U.S. Cavalry. Place and date: At Chiricahua Mountains, Ariz., 29 October 1869. Entered service at: —. Birth: Columbus, Ohio. Date of issue: 14 February 1870.
Citation: Gallantry in action
[Marker says his rank was corporal.]

In Grateful Memory of Our Fallen Soldiers

On Memorial Day, American flags festoon the gravestones at Nashville National Cemetery and re-enactors honor those who fought in our country's wars.

United States Colored Troops
Nashville National Cemetery

During a war fought to free African-Americans in bondage it is often forgotten that free blacks and freed slaves fought as soldiers in the U.S. Army during the Civil War. Known as the U.S. Colored Troops, nearly 24,000 men of color served in the U.S. forces in Tennessee and suffered 4,500 casualties. They comprised 22 infantry regiments and eight artillery units.

Commemorating the role of the USCT in the war is the lifesize bronze statue of a USCT infantryman dedicated in 2006 at Nashville's National Cemetery, the site of many USCT burials. The sculptor was Roy Butler. The model for the sculpture was William Radcliff, a USCT re-enactor.

Both slaves and freemen were used by Confederates and Unionists to erect fortifications, drive horse and mule teams, and other menial tasks. African-Americans built most of the Union fortifications around Nashville, including Fort Negley. In 1863, however, Union authorities began enlisting blacks into all-colored infantry and artillery units, commanded by white officers. Initially these units were used to garrison forts such as Fort Negley or to protect railroad bridges and trestles.

Several USCT units fought in the Battle of Nashville. On the first day USCT units assaulted the right flank of the Confederate line and marched into an ambush in which scores were killed. On the second day, USCT units, along with others, attacked Peach Orchard Hill and again suffered many casualties. The 13th USCT Regiment reached the parapets of the hill, losing five regimental flagbearers in succession and a total of 220 men. Although these troops were inexperienced, they fought bravely. One Confederate general cited their bravery in his afterbattle report.

Spring Hill Cemetery Walking Tour Map

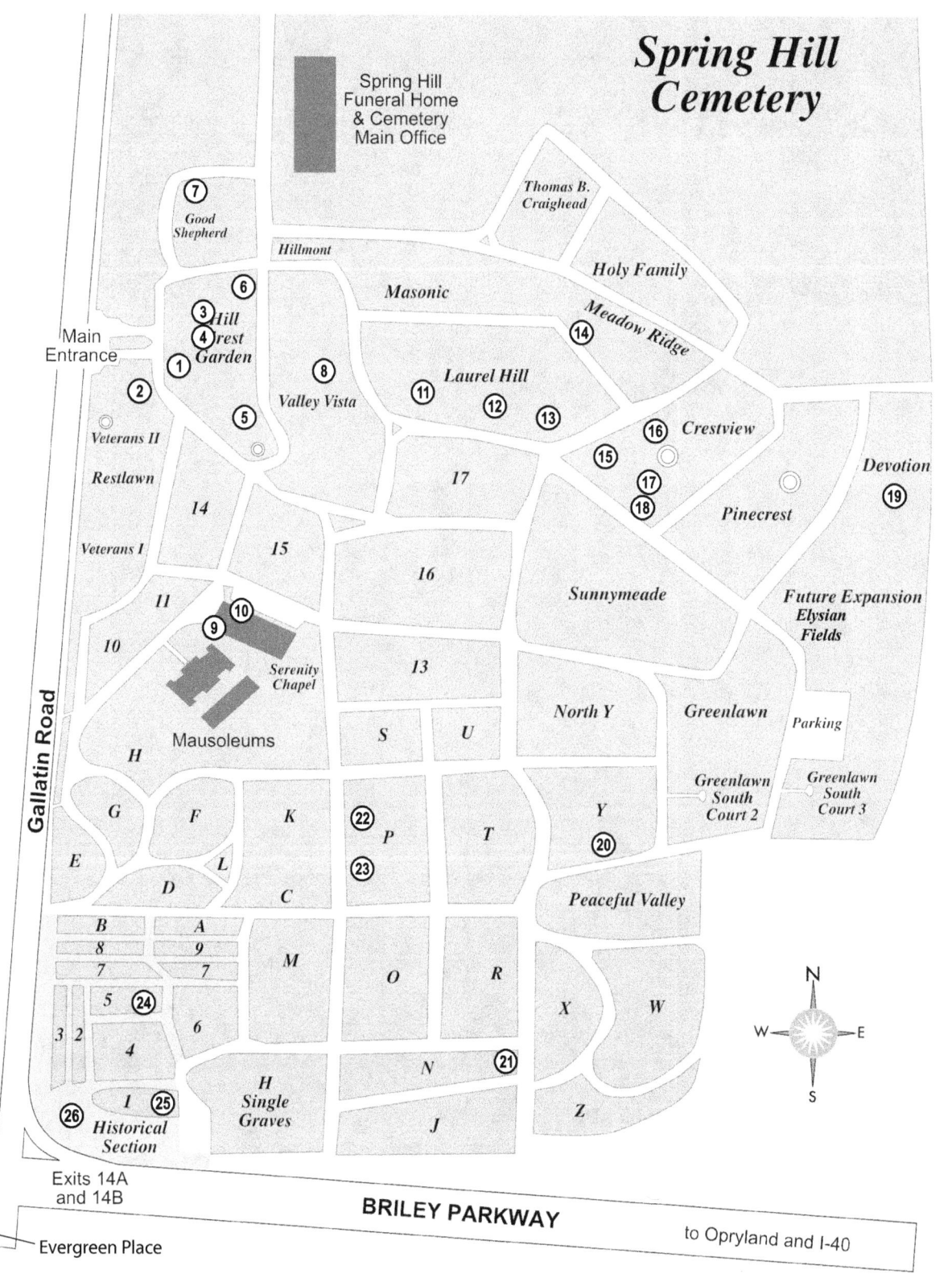

Spring Hill Cemetery

Spring Hill Cemetery is located at 5110 Gallatin Road in Madison, directly across the street from the Nashville National Cemetery. It is one of the largest and most important historic cemeteries in Middle Tennessee, founded in 1785. In addition, many of Nashville's country music stars are buried here. Also buried here is Madison Stratton, for whom Madison is named.

In 1785, the founding settlers of Nashville persuaded Thomas B. Craighead, a Presbyterian minister and Princeton graduate, to relocate here with the promise of 640 acres of land. Under his direction, the Spring Hill Meeting House, a 20x30 stone building, was constructed which became not only the first church in the area but the first school. In 1785 the government of North Carolina established Davidson Academy at this site, the first school west of the Cumberland Mountains. The school later evolved into the University of Nashville. The church's graveyard eventually became Spring Hill Cemetery. The meeting house does not exist anymore. Craighead's nearby homes, Evergreen Place and Glen Echo, were demolished in recent years by commercial construction. Buried here are many famous country music stars and longtime members of the *Grand Ole Opry*, including Roy Acuff, Kitty Wells, Jimmy Martin, Billy Walker, Pete Drake, John Hartford, George Morgan, and Keith Whitley. The historical portion of the cemetery is located in the southwest corner of the property.

Roy Acuff's monument depicts his favorite instrument.

In the historical section of the cemetery are the markers for early pioneer Thomas Stratton, his wife Elizabeth, and son Madison. The area of Nashville in which Spring Hill Cemetery is located is called Madison.

① **Roy Claxton Acuff** (1903-1992), the "King of Country Music," was one of the most beloved performers on the *Grand Ole Opry*, having debuted in 1938 singing "The Great Speckled Bird." In 1942 Acuff and Fred Rose established the famous Acuff-Rose music publishing company. In 1962 Acuff was the first living artist elected to the Country Music Hall of Fame. He grew up in East Tennessee and played fiddle on local radio and for a traveling medicine show. Acuff and his group, The Crazy Tennesseans, recorded songs in Chicago, Ill. in 1936 and auditioned successfully for the *Grand Ole Opry* in 1938, performing a wildly popular version of "The Great Speckled Bird" gospel tune. He changed the name of his group to The Smokey Mountain Boys. Hosting the *Opry* on the NBC Radio Network made Acuff a national star. In 1946 he left the *Opry*, toured the West Coast, and starred in seven Hollywood movies. Although he returned to the *Opry*, he also toured, until a near-fatal accident in 1965.

In addition to songwriting and performing, Acuff published his own songbooks. In 1942 he teamed with Fred Rose (1897-1954), a gifted songwriter and talent scout, to form Acuff-Rose Publications. Rose was instrumental in moving the Nashville music scene from folk-country to a more commercial pop-country format. The company signed Hank Williams and many other stars; their first major pop hit was "The Tennessee Waltz," performed by Patti Page in 1950.

In 1948 he was nominated by the Republicans for governor of Tennessee but lost the general election. In 1974 the *Opry* moved from downtown Nashville to the new modern Opryhouse in the suburbs. On opening night, Acuff hosted the show with special guest President Richard Nixon, who played the piano and tried to learn some yo-yo tricks from Acuff. After the death of his wife Mildred in 1981, Acuff lived on the Opryland grounds until his death.

② **Jimmy Martin** (1927-2005). Erected before his death, the gravestone of Jimmy Martin, the "King of Bluegrass," contains a detailed biography of the native East Tennessean. Martin often had his picture taken beside the monument. A tenor, he was the lead vocalist for Bill Monroe's Blue Grass Boys for much of 1949-1953. Known for his "High Lonesome" sound in his hit songs of the 1950s and 1960s, he was instrumental in bringing bluegrass music into the mainstream. Martin enjoyed a comeback playing with The Nitty Gritty Dirt Band on the *Will the Circle Be Unbroken* album, which was released in 1971.

③ **Earl Scruggs** (1924-2012) was the world's most famous banjo player. He died March 28, 2012 in Nashville at the age of 88. His funeral was conducted at the famed Ryman Auditorium. Born in 1924 in North Carolina, Scruggs played banjo in Bill Monroe's Blue Grass Boys using his three-finger picking style and teamed up with fellow bandmember Lester Flatt to form the Foggy Mountain Boys, later Flatt and Scruggs. They broke up in 1969. Although world-class bluegrass musicians, they are probably best known for playing the theme song for the 1960s' TV sitcom *The Beverly Hillbillies*. He won several Grammy awards, including the Lifetime Achievement Award. He is a member of the Country Music Hall of Fame. His wife, Louise, who died in 2006, was his business manager, the first woman to serve in that capacity in the country music business.

The impressive monument of Earl and Louise Scruggs tells the stories of their lives together, their accomplishments, and depictions of the stages of their lives and careers.

④ **Kitty Wells** (1919-2012), the Queen of Country Music, died July 16, 2012 in Madison at the age of 92. Born Ellen Muriel Deason, in Nashville, on Aug. 30, 1919, she created the role for all other female country singers. "It Wasn't God Who Made Honky Tonk Angels," recorded in 1952, was her first number one song; she was the first female to sell a million records and reach number one in the country field. She learned to play guitar at age 14 and learned to love country music from her father, Charles Cary Deason, a brakeman for the Tennessee Central Railroad who played banjo and guitar. In 1937, Kitty married Johnny Wright (1914-2011), who was half of the famous duo Johnny and Jack (Jack Anglin was married to Johnny's sister, Louise). Later, Johnny was famous for his song, "Hello Vietnam." Her marker is titled Muriel Wright; the location is unspecified.

⑤ **Clarence "Hank" Snow** (1914-1999), a native of Nova Scotia, Canada, was known as the "Singing Ranger." He joined the *Grand Ole Opry* in 1950 and performed for 46 years. His song "I'm Moving On" was the top country song of 1950 and holds the record for most consecutive weeks at No. 1. He helped discover Elvis Presley. Abused as a child, he founded the Hank Snow Foundation to help abused children. He was elected to the Country Music Hall of Fame in 1979.

⑥ **Bill Monroe Family.** Family members of Bill Monroe (1911-1996), the "Father of Bluegrass Music," are buried here—wife Carolyn Minnie (1913-1984) and daughter Melissa Kathleen (1936-1990). Monroe himself is buried in Rosine, Ky.

⑦ **Howard Forrester** (1922-1987). Known as Big Howdy, Forrester was an old-time fiddle player who played with the Tennessee Valley Boys, Bill Monroe's Bluegrass Boys, and for 36 years on the *Grand Ole Opry* with Roy Acuff's Smokey Mountain Boys. He is known as one of the greatest fiddlers of all time. (Burial near tree in corner.)

⑧ **David M. "Bunny" Biggs** (1897-1948) performed on the *Grand Ole Opry* radio show as Jamup of the Jamup and Honey comedy team during the 1940s. Holdovers from the minstrel show era, the "Assassins of Sorrow" performed in blackface and anchored the first touring tent show under *Opry* auspices. Honey was performed by Lee Wilds.

⑨ **Mary Reeves Davis** (1929-1999) was the wife of "Gentleman Jim" Reeves, a talented vocalist who enjoyed great fame as a country-pop music crooner and adherent of the Nashville Sound. Reeves, a pilot, died tragically in 1964 at age 40 in an airplane crash near Nashville and is buried in his native Texas. Mary Reeves worked hard to keep her husband's legacy alive, opening a museum to his memory at nearby Evergreen Place. From 1964 to 1970 Jim Reeves had 14 consecutive top-ten hits. A prolific world traveler during his lifetime, Reeves remains a huge fan favorite in many foreign countries. (Inside Serenity Chapel at northwest end.)

⑩ **Roy M. Huskey Jr.** (1956-1997). He was Nashville's premier acoustic bassist and a member of the Nash Ramblers, Emmylou Harris' band. He began at age 16 backing up Del Wood on the *Opry* in 1971. He toured with Roy Acuff's Smoky Mountain Boys and performed with Chet Atkins, Garth Brooks, and Johnny Cash, among many others. He died of lung cancer at age 40. He was the son of noted musician Junior Huskey. (Inside Serenity Chapel at northwest end.)

⑪ **R.F. "Pete" Drake** (1932-1988) was an outstanding pedal steel guitarist, playing on hundreds of recordings, including those by country stars Johnny Cash and Dolly Parton and pop stars Elvis, George Harrison, and Bob Dylan. His style of "talking guitar" crossed the gap between country and popular music. He performed on "Behind Closed Doors" by Charlie Rich, "Stand By Your Man" by Tammy Wynette, and "Rose Garden" by Lynn Anderson. He is a member of the Country Music Hall of Fame.

⑫ **Billy Walker** (1929-2006), the "Tall Texan," was a well-loved regular of the *Grand Ole Opry* and had six No. 1 hits and 32 in the Top Ten. Two of his biggest hits were "Charlie's Shoes" and "Funny How Time Slips Away" in the early 1960s. Due to a last-minute emergency, he narrowly avoided the 1963 airplane flight that took the life of Patsy Cline and entourage. He and his devoted wife Bettie died in an automobile accident in Alabama in 2006.

⑬ **Curt Gibson** (1926-2006) was a guitar player and disc jockey from Alabama who co-wrote songs with George Morgan and others. He was 17 when he first aired on WLAC radio in Nashville. He worked with Stringbean Akeman. He started his own publishing company, Curt Gibson Music, and played in Hank Snow's band from 1974 to 1986.

⑭ **Gilbert "Speck" Rhodes** (1915-2000). A native of Missouri, he formed a comedic duo with Cousin Jody and performed for many years on *The Porter Wagoner Show*. He played banjo and bass fiddle with his musical family, the Log Cabin Mountaineers, on the vaudeville circuit in the 1930s.

⑮ **George T. Morgan** (1924-1975). A smooth country crooner best known for his debut hit "Candy Kisses" (1949), Morgan replaced Eddy Arnold on the *Grand Ole Opry* in 1948 and enjoyed many years of success. Following "Candy Kisses," he had six more hits in the top ten during 1949. His

Gone Under • *Historic Cemeteries of Nashville, Tennessee – 2nd Edition*

Clarence "Hank" Snow (1914-1999) was a native of Nova Scotia, Canada, and known as the "Singing Ranger." He played on the Grand Ole Opry for 46 years and his song "I'm Moving On" was the top country song of 1950 and holds the record for most consecutive weeks at No. 1.

Billy Walker, the "Tall Texan," was a well-loved regular of the Grand Ole Opry and had six No. 1 hits and 32 in the Top Ten. Due to a last-minute emergency, he narrowly avoided the 1963 airplane flight that took the life of Patsy Cline. He and his devoted wife Bettie died in an auto accident in Alabama in 2006.

Country Music Stars

The gravestone of Jimmy Martin, the "King of Bluegrass," contains a complete biography. He was known for his "High Lonesome" sound in his hit songs of the 1950s and 1960s.

Pete Drake (1932-1988) was an outstanding pedal steel guitarist, playing on hundreds of recordings, including those of Elvis, George Harrison, and Bob Dylan. His style of "talking guitar" crossed the gap between country and popular music. He is a member of the Country Music Hall of Fame.

J. Keith Whitley (1955-1989), a native of Kentucky, learned to play guitar at age six and later as a teenager formed a bluegrass band with friend Ricky Skaggs. Ralph Stanley hired them for his band. Whitley would go on to release several hit albums and songs and became a very popular performer. Tragically, Whitley died of alcohol poisoning at age 33. The burial plot includes a place for his widow, Lorrie Morgan, the daughter of singer George Morgan, who is buried nearby.

daughter, Lorrie Morgan, born in 1959, also earned a spot on the *Opry*. His posthumous father-daughter duet, "I'm Completely Satisfied with You," was released in 1979.

⑯ **J. Keith Whitley** (1955-1989), a native of Kentucky, learned to play guitar at age six and later as a teenager formed a bluegrass band with his friend Ricky Skaggs. Ralph Stanley hired them for his band. Whitley would go on to release several hit albums and songs and became a popular performer. He hit No. 1 in 1988 with "Don't Close Your Eyes." His "When You Say Nothing at All" has become a wedding standard. Tragically, Whitley died of alcohol poisoning at age 33. His burial plot includes a place for his widow, Lorrie Morgan, the daughter of singer George Morgan, who is buried nearby. She was born in 1959. They were married in 1986. His marker reads "His Being Was My Reason."

⑰ **Dockie Dean Manuel** (1934-1964). Manuel was singer Jim Reeves' manager and piano player, and was killed along with Reeves in a 1964 plane crash near Nashville. The two men had looked at investment property in Batesville, Ark. (where Manuel had grown up) and were returning home in bad weather when their small plane disappeared on July 31. It took two days to find the wreckage in Brentwood, Tenn.

⑱ **Clifton Beverly Briley Sr.** (1914-1980) served as the first mayor of metropolitan Nashville-Davidson County from 1963-1975. A local native and conservative Democrat, he helped move the city away from racial segregationist policies during the early 1960s. Previously he had been a successful lawyer (at age 18 the youngest person admitted to the bar in Tennessee) and county judge of Davidson County from 1950 to 1963. Briley Parkway, which borders the cemetery, is named for him. His marker bears the Metro Seal.

⑲ **John Hartford** (1937-2001). Best known as the writer of megahit "Gentle On My Mind," Hartford displayed a multitude of talents, especially on the fiddle and banjo, and played on many albums. He was born John Harford in New York City and grew up in St. Louis, Mo. on the Mississippi River. Later in life, he earned a riverboat pilot's license. In 1965 he moved to Nashville and was a DJ at WSIX radio. He was a proponent of progressive bluegrass and the modern jam band movement. During one period in the 1970s he moved to Los Angeles and appeared on many TV variety shows. He released several eclectic solo albums on the Flying Fish label, including *Mark Twang* (1976), which won a Grammy for Best Traditional Recording. For years before his death, he battled with non-Hodgkin's lymphoma.

EVERGREEN PLACE—The Rev. Thomas Brown Craighead settled this land in 1795. He was a prominent Presbyterian minister and founding father of Davidson Academy, now known as Cumberland College. A.W. Johnson, a wealthy local merchant, purchased the property from the Craigheads in 1845, after Mrs. Craighead's death. Johnson built a two-story dogtrot log cabin at the site, and tests indicate the original logs for the cabin were harvested in 1837. The cabin was later remodeled into a wood frame and brick Tennessee vernacular farmhouse. It is unknown if the farmhouse was remodeled by Johnson or Mr. and Mrs. Carlos and Narcissa Demick, who bought the property in 1854. Mrs. Demick is given credit for naming the property Evergreen Place. In 1855, Mr. Demick and his two children died of consumption. In 1857, Narcissa married George Bradford, a Civil War veteran. Bradford died in 1866, and Narcissa lived the remainder of her life at Evergreen Place until her death in 1896. The Bradfords raised six children together. George Bradford, Jr., one of their sons, made Evergreen Place famous for Jersey Cattle in the early 1900s. In 1980, the descendants of the Bradford family sold Evergreen Place to Mary Reeves Davis, the widow of country-western singer Jim Reeves. The property then became the home of the Jim Reeves Museum for approximately ten years. Evergreen Place was demolished in 2005. These two log structures are all that remain. They are located behind the Regions Bank in the southwest quadrant of the Briley Parkway-Gallatin Road interchange.

The crypt of Rev. Thomas B. Craighead and wife Elizabeth is located in Spring Hill Cemetery at the site of the original meeting-house graveyard. The small obelisk is dedicated to their only daughter, Jane. In the background can be seen the Gallatin Road overpass of Briley Parkway.

⑳ **Floyd Cramer** (1933-1997). A member of the Country Music Hall of Fame, Cramer was an influential piano player and teamed up often with Chet Atkins, Patsy Cline, and Roy Orbison. Two of his best songs were "On the Rebound" and "New San Antonio Rose." He can also be heard on songs by Elvis Presley ("Heartbreak Hotel") and Jim Reeves ("Four Walls"). He performed the theme song to the hit TV series *Dallas*.

㉑ **Beth Slater Whitson** (1879-1930). From Happy Hollow in Hickman County, Whitson was a prolific writer, penning "Meet Me Tonight in Dreamland" in 1909 and co-writing "Let Me Call You Sweetheart" in 1910 with her younger sister Alice Whitson Norton (1885-1961), who is buried nearby. Whitson had 200 songs published and also wrote poems and short stories. She and her sister moved to Nashville in 1913.

㉒ **Charles F. "Red" Lucas** (1902-1986). A right-handed professional pitcher for the New York Giants, Boston Braves, Cincinnati Reds, and Pittsburgh Pirates, Lucas set the modern record for pitching 250 $\frac{1}{3}$ consecutive innings (27 complete games) in 1931-32. He played for 15 seasons. He led the National League in pinch hitting four times (batting from the left). Babe Ruth hit his 712th home run off Lucas on May 25, 1935 (Ruth's last two homers came later in that same game). Lucas was a native of Columbia, Tenn. He was called "The Nashville Narcissus." He bought a house in Nashville in 1930 and lived there the rest of his life.

㉓ **Gerald M. Rivers** (1928-1996). A native of Miami, Fla., Jerry "Burrhead" Rivers grew up in Nashville. He played fiddle with the Drifting Cowboys, Hank Williams' band, beginning in 1949, when Williams came to Nashville. Previously he worked with Big Jeff Bess. In 1964 he released *Fantastic Fiddlin' and Tall Tales*, followed by *A New Frontier* in 1967 with his new band The Homesteaders. That year his book *Hank Williams: From Life to Legend* was published. In 1977, the Drifting Cowboys reformed and toured with Jett Williams and appeared in the movie *That's Country*.

㉔ **Madison Stratton** (1813-1894). Early settler who gave the suburb of Madison its name. In 1850, he sold land to be used for the Madison train depot. His father, Thomas Stratton, came from Virginia to the Haysborough area in 1809. In 1857 the community was renamed Madison Station (a stop on the Edgefield and Kentucky Railroad) in his honor. The railroad station, later named Amqui Station, was purchased and relocated by country superstar Johnny Cash. In 2003, the building was relocated back to Madison. An unincorporated section of Davidson County, Madison claimed a population of 37,316 in the 2010 census.

㉕ **Rev. Thomas B. Craighead** (1750-1825). The Rev. Craighead, a graduate of Princeton University in New Jersey, came to Nashville in 1785 at the request of the founding fathers and became Nashville's first preacher. He established his residence at Spring Hill on 640 acres and founded the first church, whose graveyard eventually became Spring Hill Cemetery, and the first school, which was organized as Davidson Academy, the predecessor to the University of Nashville. A Presbyterian, Craighead was controversial for his "liberal beliefs," such as the role of human free will in spiritual salvation.

㉖ **History of Spring Hill Cemetery Plaque.** "The Spring Hill Meeting House was built here in 1785. The church yard was used as a community burying ground. In 1813, this was conveyed to a Board of Commissioners and designated to be used as a burying ground forever. It was called Craighead Spring Hill Cemetery. In 1881, the state issued a charter for the incorporation of Spring Hill Cemetery. Thomas Craighead, the first preacher and teacher at Spring Hill Meeting House is buried nearby in the church yard."

Woodlawn Memorial Gardens Walking Tour

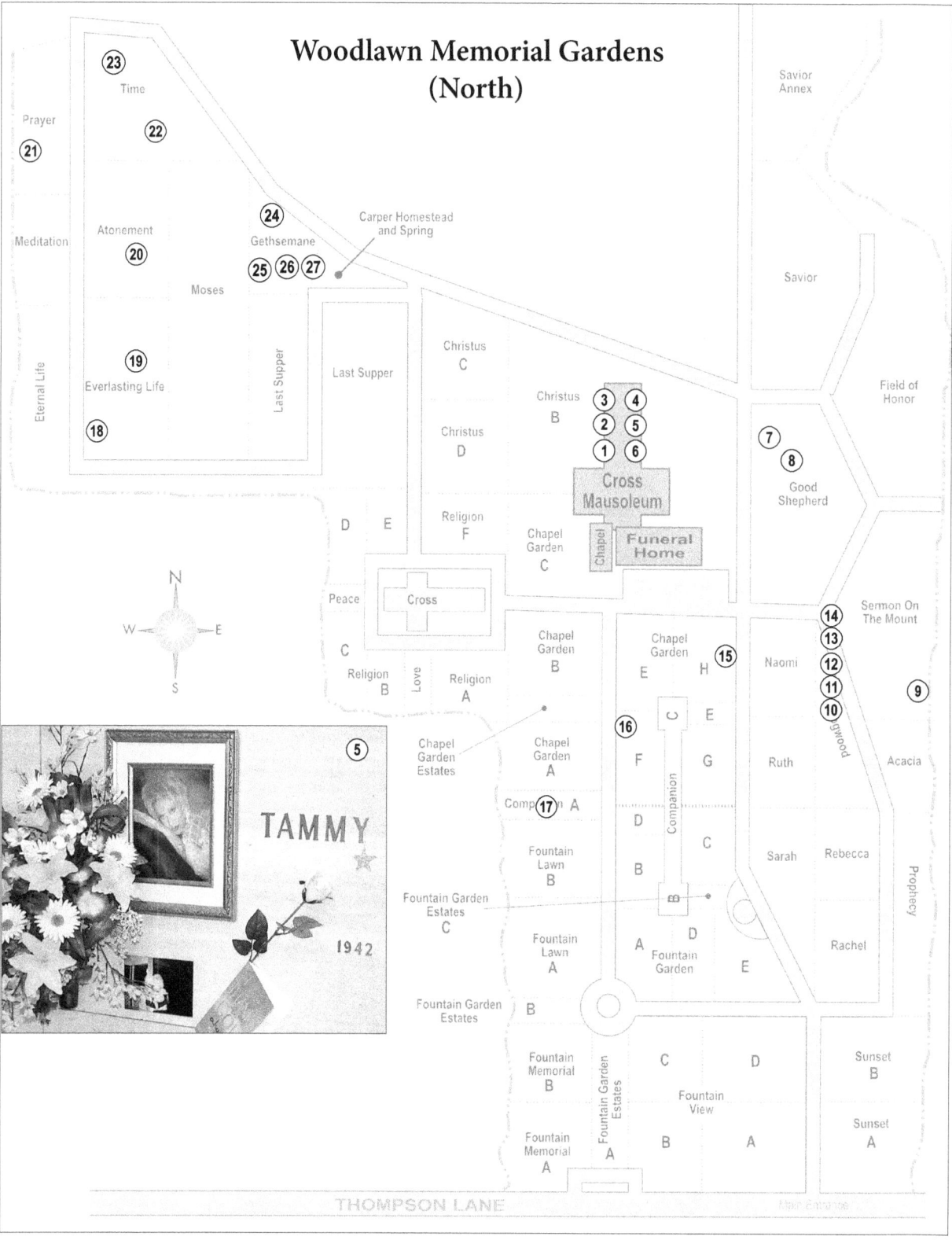

Woodlawn Memorial Gardens

Woodlawn Memorial Gardens is located at 660 Thompson Lane. The phone is (615) 383-4754.

① **Van Stephenson** (1953-2001) was a singer-songwriter who was the tenor vocalist and lead guitarist in the country music band BlackHawk, which he co-founded in 1992. Prior to that, he was a solo artist and wrote several hit songs for the group Restless Heart. He died of cancer at age 47. (North Cross Mausoleum-3rd Floor-252C).

② **Jack Stapp** (1912-1980) was the program director of Nashville radio station WSM from 1939 to 1957 and founder of Tree Publishing Company. He was instrumental in securing talent for the *Grand Ole Opry* in the 1940s and 1950s. He was elected to the Country Music Hall of Fame in 1989. (East Cross Mausoleum-2nd Floor-172C).

③ **Boudleaux Bryant** (1920-1987) and **Felice Bryant** (1925-2003) were the husband-and-wife songwriting team who wrote 1,500 recorded songs which sold 300 million copies. A native of Georgia, Boudleaux was named after a Frenchman who saved his father's life in World War One. Among their notable songs were "Bye Bye Love," "Wake Up Little Susie," "Blue Boy," and "Rocky Top." They were elected to the Country Music Hall of Fame in 1991. (North Cross Mausoleum-3rd Floor).

④ **John Daniel "J.D." Sumner** (1924-1998) was the leader of J.D. Sumner and the Stamps, which toured and recorded with Elvis Presley from 1971 until his death in 1977. He performed with the Masters V group in the 1980s. Sumner, a bass singer, was also the co-founder of the National Quartet Convention and the Gospel Music Association, which recognizes achievements through the Dove Awards. (North Cross Mausoleum-3rd Floor-383 B-B1).

⑤ **Tammy Wynette** (1942-1998), born Virginia Wynette Pugh in Mississippi, was the "First Lady of Country Music," elected to the Country Music Hall of Fame shortly after her death. Divorced and with three children, she moved to Nashville in 1966 and produced ten No. 1 hits with Epic producer Billy Sherrill. She sang about real-life women's issues and her biggest hit was "Stand By Your Man." She and second husband George Jones produced a string of hit duets. Their marriage, sometimes stormy, lasted from 1969 to 1975. In 1993 she joined Dolly Parton and Loretta Lynn in recording the *Honky Tonk Angels* album. Her funeral service was televised from the Ryman Auditorium. (North Cross Mausoleum-3rd Floor 274-275B).

⑥ **Little Jimmy Dickens** (1920-2015), born James Cecil Dickens in West Virginia, was a country music singer and songwriter famous for his humorous novelty songs, his 4'11" shortness, and his flashy rhinestone-studded outfits. He started as a member of the *Grand Ole Opry* in 1948 (having been discovered by Roy Acuff) and was inducted into the Country Music Hall of Fame in 1983. At his death at age 94, he was the oldest living member of the *Grand Ole Opry*. (Cross Mausoleum).

⑦ **Jackson Brock Speer** (1920-1999) became the leader of the Singing Speer Family after his parents passed away in 1966 and 1967. He lent the group his smooth bass voice. He also served as president of the Gospel Music Association. He and his family group are members of the GMA Hall of Fame. (Good Shepherd-Lot 240-A #1).

⑧ **Woodrow Wilson "Red" Sovine** (1918-1980) Country music and *Grand Ole Opry* star known for his truck-driving songs, including "Teddy Bear," which hit No. 1 in 1976. He replaced Hank Williams on the *Louisiana Hayride* when Williams went to Nashville. He persuaded Charley Pride to go to Nashville and start his career. (Good Shepherd-Lot 111-C #1).

⑨ **Claudette Orbison** (1941-1966), Anthony King Orbison (1962-1968) and Roy Dewayne Orbison (1958-1968). Claudette Orbison was vocalist Roy Orbison's first wife and the inspiration for one of his most famous songs. She died in a 1966 motorcycle accident in Gallatin, Tenn. In 1968, two of Orbison's three young sons died in a house fire in Hendersonville, Tenn. while he was touring in England. Also buried here is Orbison's older brother Grady Lee (1933-1973), who died in a car accident. Orbison himself died in 1988 and is buried in Westwood, Calif. (Sermon on the Mount-Lot 49C).

⑩ **George Jones** (1931-2013), also known as the Possum, was arguably the finest country music male vocalist and songwriter of all time. His string of top hits during four decades (1950s-1980s) included "Just One More," "White Lightnin'," "She Thinks I Still Care," "Walk Though This World With Me," "The Grand Tour," and "He Stopped Loving Her Today." He was heavily influenced by singer/songwriter Hank Williams. He charted more than 150 times. A native Texan and US Marine Corps veteran, Jones was also known for his turbulent marriage to singing partner Tammy Wynette (1969-1973) and his bouts with alcohol and drugs. In the 1980s he returned to his honky-tonk roots and established a stable fourth marriage. In 1998 he began hosting his own variety show on TNN, *The George Jones Show*, which ran for two years. He is a member of the Country Music Hall of Fame. (Garden of the Grand Tour).

George Jones, one of the greatest vocalists and songwriters of all time, was also known as The Possum. His monument can be found at the Garden of the Grand Tour.

Rob Baronis was an All-Pro placekicker for the Tennesssee Titans.

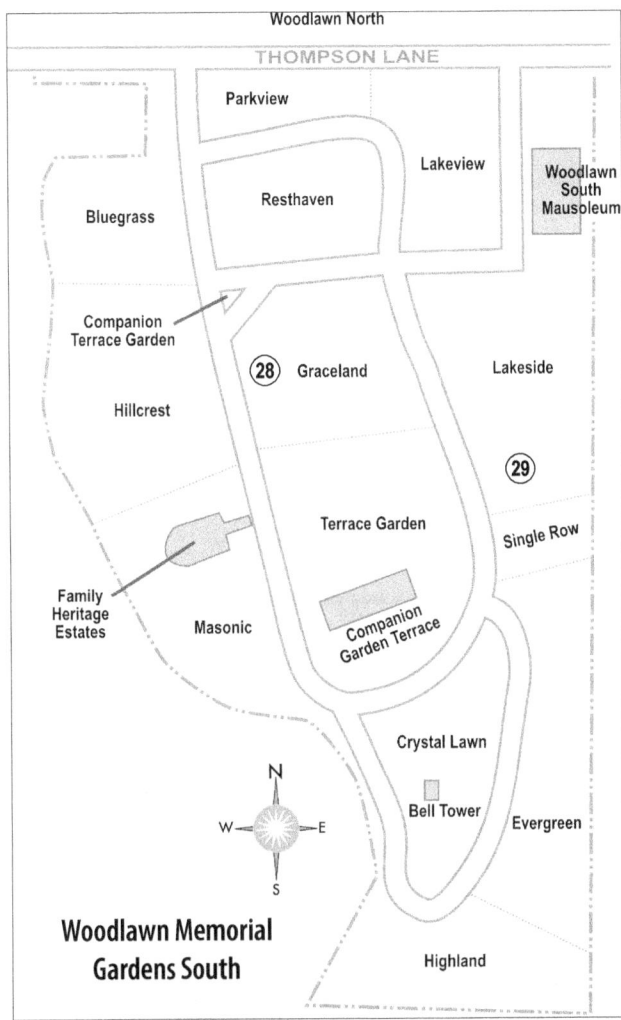

⑪ Johnny Paycheck or **PayCheck** (1938-2003) is best remembered for his 1977 hit song "Take This Job and Shove It." He recorded over 70 albums. He was born Donald E. Lytle in Greenfield, Ohio. "The Ohio Kid" joined the U.S. Navy and was court-martialed for striking an officer, serving two years in military prison. In Nashville, he played in bands for Porter Wagoner, Ray Price, Faron Young, and George Jones. He legally changed his name in the mid-1960s (the original Paycheck was a boxer). He had a string of hits in the 1970s but also struggled in his personal life. Convicted of a shooting in a barroom brawl, he served two years in prison in 1989-1991. He emerged clean and sober, and in 1997 was invited to join the *Grand Ole Opry*. (Garden of the Grand Tour).

⑫ James Robert Douglas "Rob" Baronis (1978-2014) was a National Football League placekicker with the Tennessee Titans. He holds the NFL record for field goals in a single game (8), set in 2007 against the Houston Texans. Bironas was an All-Pro and Pro Bowl selection in 2007. He was married to the daughter of Hall of Fame quarterback Terry Bradshaw. He was killed in a car crash in Nashville on Sept. 20, 2014. (Garden of the Grand Tour).

⑬ Billy Sherrill (1936-2015) was a Nashville record producer, songwriter, and arranger best known for his association with Tammy Wynette and George Jones. He produced hits using the crossover style of the "Nashville Sound." Sherrill also co-wrote many hit songs, including "Stand by Your Man" (written with Wynette) and "The Most Beautiful Girl" (written with Rory Bourke and Norro Wilson). In 1980, he was appointed as Vice President of CBS in Nashville. He is a member of the Country Music Hall of Fame. (Garden of the Grand Tour).

⑭ Jerry Chesnut (1931 – 2018) was the 1972 US National Songwriter of the Year and the 1973 International Songwriter of the Year. His hits include "A Good Year for the Roses" (recorded by Alan Jackson and George Jones) and "T-R-O-U-B-L-E" (recorded by Elvis Presley and Travis Tritt). In 1968 Jerry Lee Lewis's recording of Chesnut's "Another Place, Another Time" was nominated for a Grammy Award. He is a member of the Nashville Songwriters Hall of Fame. (Garden of the Grand Tour).

⑮ Richard Edward "Eddy" Arnold (1918-2008), a silky voiced crooner known as the "Tennessee Plowboy," typified the more sophisticated Nashville Sound of the 1960s and was named the first CMA Entertainer of the Year in 1967. Earlier, during a 14-month period in 1947-1949, Arnold had six No. 1 songs and in late 1948 he had six songs in the top ten at one time. Two of his most famous songs are "Make the World Go Away" and "What's He Doing in My World." He was elected to the Country Music Hall of Fame in 1966. He appeared on the *Grand Ole Opry* and many TV shows and made country music accessible to middle-class listeners. Upon his death, there were public services at the Country Music Hall of Fame and the Ryman Auditorium. (Chapel Garden H).

⑯ William Owen Bradley (1915-1998) was a pioneer of the country music recording industry, developer of the Nashville Sound, and producer for Loretta Lynn, Conway Twitty, Kitty Wells, and Patsy Cline. The Owen Bradley Orchestra was once considered the premier Nashville dance band. The heart of the Music City USA business district is Music Row, which comprises 16th and 17th avenues between Grand and Division. This district contains 180 studios, 130 music publishers, and 80 record labels. At the head of Music Row is Owen Bradley Park, featuring a bronze sculpture of Bradley seated at a piano. In 1954, Owen and brother Harold Bradley built a recording studio at 804 16th Avenue in an old Quonset hut built by the military during World War Two. The Bradleys recorded songs performed by Hank Williams, Kitty

Clockwise from above: Owen Bradley, the founder of Music Row and co-founder of the "Nashville Sound." • Larrie Londin, prolific sessions drummer, his grave marker lists 117 names of artists he accompanied. • The incredibly talented Marty Robbins. • Webb Pierce, the "Wondering Boy". • Martha Carson, the "First Lady of Gospel Music." • Hattie L. Bess, the owner-operator of Tootsie's Orchid Lounge on Lower Broadway. • Johnny Paycheck, whose big hit was "Take This Job and Shove It."

Wells, Webb Pierce, and Red Foley. Along with Chet Atkins, Bradley is credited with producing the unique crossover Nashville Sound of the 1960s that utilized string arrangements, soaring background vocals, and the use of various studio techniques. The Bradleys had previously accompanied Snooky Lanson at a recording session at Castle Studio, the first recording studio in Nashville. Three WSM radio engineers opened the studio in 1945 inside the Tulane Hotel. (WSM radio called itself the Air Castle of the South.) Recording at the studio were artists such as the Everly Brothers, Burl Ives, Kitty Wells, and Red Foley. (Chapel Garden F-Lot 19 #2).

⑰ **Thomas Lee "Tommy" Jackson** (1926-1979) was one of the greatest Nashville sessions fiddlers. He recorded with Hank Williams, Bill Monroe, and George Jones, among others, and appeared on the *Grand Ole Opry*, beginning at age 17. He had toured at age 12 with John Wright and Kitty Wells. During WWII, he earned four Bronze Stars as a tailgunner in a B-29 bomber. He became a member of Red Foley's band, the Cumberland Valley Boys. From 1953 to 1963 he recorded many albums of square dance music. He also played fiddle for Ray Price and Faron Young. (Companion Guardian A-Lot 40 #2).

⑱ **Dale T. "Stoney" Cooper** (1918-1977) was a fiddler and vocalist from West Virginia who performed with his wife as Wilma Lee and Stoney Cooper. They joined the Opry in 1954 after ten years with the rival Wheeling (W.Va.) Jamboree. They had four top ten bluegrass hits from 1956 to 1961. Wilma sang in her youth with her family's gospel music group, The Leary Family. (Everlasting Life-Lot 120-D #1).

⑲ **Porter Wagoner** (1927-2007) was the grand master of the *Grand Ole Opry*, having joined in 1957 with the Wagonmasters as his backing band. He also hosted his own TV show from 1960 to 1981, introducing a new female singer by the name of Dolly Parton. The singing duo of Wagoner and Parton scored a series of top ten hits from 1968 to 1975. A native of Missouri, the "Thin Man from West Plains" charted 81 records over his career. His funeral was held at the Ryman Auditorium with many Nashville performers attending. (Everlasting Life-Lot 93 B-3).

(20) **John Victor "Vic" Willis** (1922-1995) was a member of the *Grand Ole Opry's* Willis Brothers, along with Guy and Skeeter. He played accordion, piano, and sang. The group, originally called the Oklahoma Wranglers, played backup on the early Hank Williams recordings. Leaving the Opry in 1949, the group toured with Eddy Arnold until 1957. In 1964 they charted with the truck-driving song "Give Me 40 Acres (To Turn This Rig Around)." Vic Willis died in a car crash. (Garden of Atonement-Lot 34-D #3).

(21) **Hattie L. "Tootsie" Bess** (1916-1978) was the owner and proprietor from 1960 to 1978 of Tootsie's Orchid Lounge on Lower Broadway, a world-famous honky tonk saloon. She was the former wife of Big Jeff Bess, a country singer and radio performer. In 1960, Bess bought the bar known as Mom's from Louise Hackler. She was known for helping aspiring songwriters and performers such as Willie Nelson and Kris Kristofferson. Tootsie's also served as a watering hole for Opry performers, since the Ryman is just across the alleyway. Today it is a popular tourist attraction. (Prayer-Lot 101-A#1).

(22) **Mel Street** (1936-1978) was a talented hard-country music singer out of West Virginia. His biggest hit (1972) was "Lovin' On Back Streets." He suffered from depression and took his own life on his 43rd birthday. His idol, George Jones, sang at his funeral. (Time-95C #4).

(23) **Martha Carson** (1921-2004), "The First Lady of Gospel Music," was born Irene E. Amburgey in Neon, Ky. She was an energetic, red-haired singer and guitar player who charted a million-seller with her most famous song, "Satisfied," in 1951. She was a member of the *Grand Ole Opry*, sang gospel duets with Elvis, toured extensively with stars such as Patsy Cline and Del Reeves, and starred on TV shows hosted by Steve Allen and Arthur Godfrey, among others. In 1953, she married promoter Xavier Cossé. She was also known as the "Rockin' Queen of Happy Spirituals." (Gethsemane).

(24) **Willard Mack Vickery** (1938-2004) of Alabama was a Hillbilly Hall of Fame songwriter for Jerry Lee Lewis, Johnny Cash, George Jones, and George Strait, among others, and recorded the album *Live at the Alabama Women's Prison*. In the 1970s he toured with comedian Elmer Fudpucker. His "I'll Leave This World Loving You" was a hit for Ricky Van Shelton in 1989. (Gethsemane).

(25) **Webb Pierce** (1921-1991) was a hugely popular honky tonk singer in the 1950s, recording ten songs that reached No. 1 and landing 34 consecutive hits in the top ten. His most popular song was "Wondering," released in 1952. He began singing on the *Louisiana Hayride* in his native state, joined the *Grand Ole Opry* in 1952, and then left in 1955 for the *Ozark Jubilee* TV show. He was also known for his flamboyant lifestyle, which included wearing sequined Nudie suits, driving a silver dollar-lined convertible, and building a guitar-shaped swimming pool at his mansion. (Gethsemane-Lot 1-D #1).

(26) **Marty Robbins** (1925-1982), born Martin David Robinson in Arizona, was one of the most versatile and beloved singers in country and western music. He was also an avid race car driver. He joined the *Grand Ole Opry* in 1953. An early hit was "A White Sports Coat (And a Pink Carnation)" in 1957. His 1959 hit "El Paso" was the first country song awarded a Grammy and the first to hit No. 1 on the pop charts. His last crossover hit was 1970's "My Woman, My Woman, My Wife." He was the last *Opry* member to perform at the Ryman Auditorium and the first to perform at the new Opry House. Robbins was a huge fan of Hawaiian music. He also drove a NASCAR race car. In October 1982, he was inducted into the Country Music Hall of Fame. He died after his third heart attack. (Gethsemane-Lot 15-B #3).

(27) **Larrie Londin** (1943-1992), aka Ralph Gallant, was a drummer and A-team sessions player who performed for a who's who of country music and pop music, most of whom are listed on his impressive grave marker. Clients included Journey, Elvis, Hank Williams, The Supremes, and Chet Atkins. He and his brother Lonnie, who played bass, performed as The Headliners in the early 1960s and were signed by Motown Records. He died at age 48 of a heart attack. (Gethsemane-Lot 119-B #3).

(28) **Clyde J. "Red" Foley** (1910-1968) was one of the biggest singing stars in country music, selling 25 million records between 1944 and 1965. A native Kentuckian, he is credited with greatly increasing the popularity of the *Grand Ole Opry* radio show. In 1967, he was elected to the Country Music Hall of Fame. He also starred on the *National Barn Dance*, the *Renfro Valley Barn Dance*, his own network radio show, and the *Ozark Jubilee* TV show. He starred in the 1941 movie *The Pioneers* with Tex Ritter. He was the first major performer to record in Nashville. (Woodlawn South, Graceland-Lot 290 #5&6).

(29) **Grover C. "Shorty" Lavender** (1932-1982) was a fiddler who played thousands of Nashville country music recording sessions from 1955 to 1980. (Woodlawn South, Lakeside-Lot 70C #2).

Forest Lawn Memorial Gardens Walking Tour

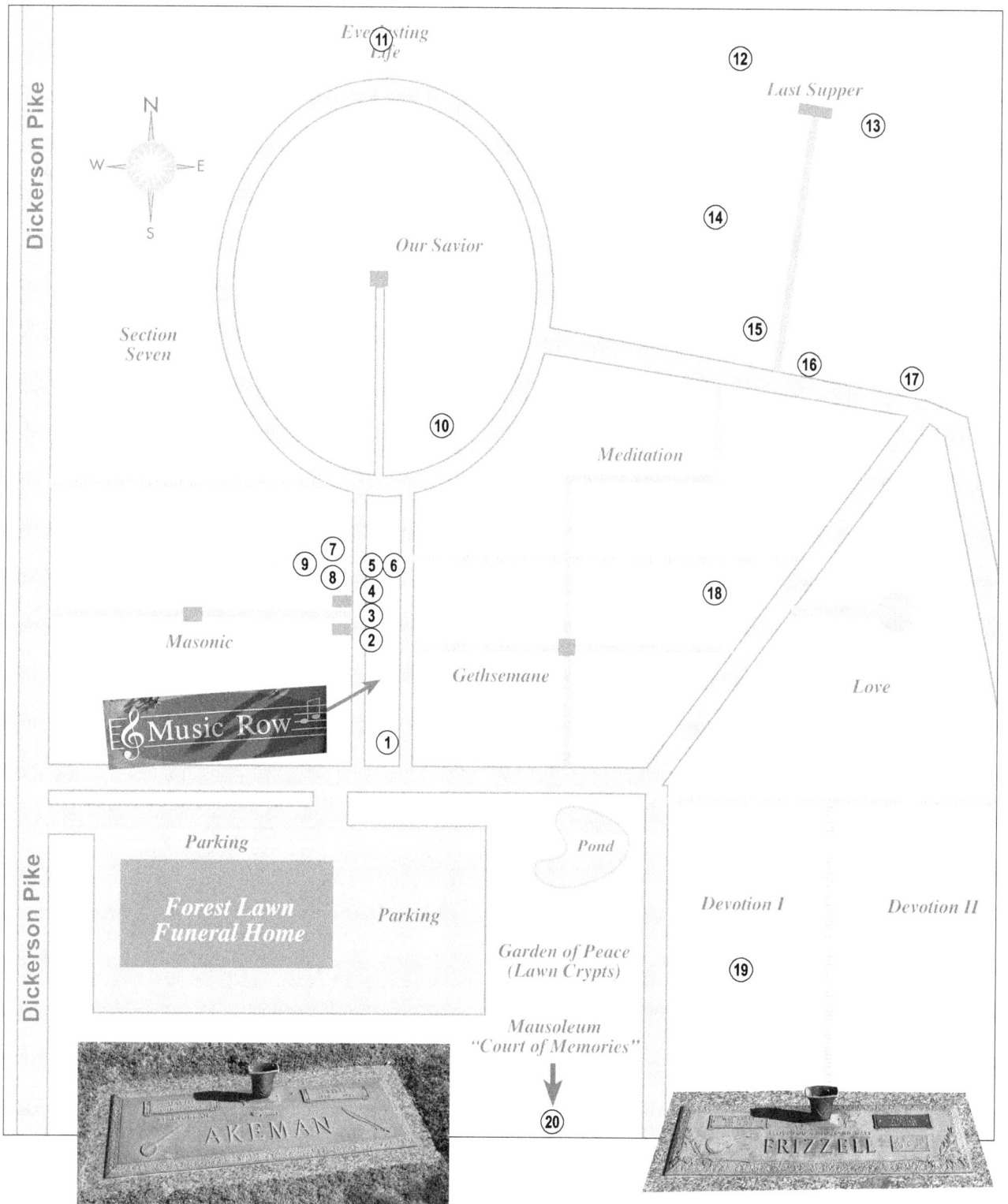

Forest Lawn Memorial Gardens

Forest Lawn Memorial Gardens is located at 1150 South Dickerson Road in Goodlettsville, Tenn., about a mile south of Goodlettsville City Hall in the northern section of Davidson County. The phone is (615) 859-5279.

Of all the cemeteries in Nashville bearing the remains of country music's stars Forest Lawn probably bears the most tragedy; the section of the cemetery known as Music Row contains the mortal remains of the victims of two of Music City's greatest tragedies—the Patsy Cline airplane crash and the Stringbean murders.

On March 5, 1963, an airplane crash near Camden, Tenn. took the lives of country singing sensation Patsy Cline and three of her entourage. Cline is buried in Virginia. Buried at Forest Lawn are **Harold F. "Hawkshaw" Hawkins** (b. 1921) ⑤, **Lloyd E. "Cowboy" Copas** (b. 1913) ⑦, and **Ramsey D. Hughes** (b. 1928) ⑧.

A West Virginian, Hawkins was loved as a singer, guitarist, songwriter, and entertainer on the *Wheeling* (W.Va.) *Jamboree*, the *Ozark Jubilee*, and the *Grand Ole Opry*. He was the husband of singer Jean Shepard. "Eleven and a Half Yards of Personality" had a rich baritone voice, an engaging style with audiences, and stood six foot six in cowboy boots. His song "Lonesome 7-7203" went to No. 1 a month after his death and became a country standard. Hawkins is buried at Music Row-10C1.

A native of Ohio, Cowboy Copas replaced Eddy Arnold as the vocalist for Pee Wee King's Golden West Cowboys on WSM-Nashville and the *Opry* in the 1940s. Cope also performed duets with his daughter Kathy. Also called "The Waltz King of the Grand Ole Opry," his cowboy nickname was obtained when he, playing flattop acoustic guitar, teamed with fiddler Lester Storer, known as "Natchee the Indian." Copas was the first artist to hit with "The Tennessee Waltz." His biggest hit was "Alabam" in 1960. He is buried at Masonic-77D1.

Randy Hughes was Patsy Cline's manager and the pilot of the aircraft. He was the son-in-law of Cowboy Copas, married to his daughter Kathy. The performers were headed back to Nashville in bad weather from a concert in Kansas City benefitting the family of DJ Cactus Jack Call, who had been killed in a car crash. Hughes is buried at Masonic-77C4.

Mourners at the March 7th service for Patsy Cline received news that *Opry* performer **Jack Anglin** (b. 1916) ⑫ had been killed in a car wreck enroute to the service. Anglin teamed with brother-in-law Johnny Wright (husband of Kitty Wells) as the Johnny & Jack singing duo, an *Opry* and touring act with a unique sound backed by the Tennessee Hillbillies, later the Tennessee Mountain Boys. Anglin is buried at Garden of the Last Supper-37C3.

⑬ **Robert L. "Bob" Foster** (1929-2000) was a noted steel guitarist who played for Cowboy Copas and Jack Anglin. (Last Supper-127A2)

⑰ **Robert Autry Inman** (1929-1988) of Alabama performed with the Cowboy Copas band The Oklahoma Cowboys and as Autry Inman and the Inmates on the *Grand Ole Opry*. He holds the record for most songs written and recorded in one year. Later in his career he switched to rockabilly music. He also wrote songs covered by Hank Williams, Johnny Cash, and Waylon Jennings. (Love-259D3)

⑥ On Nov. 10, 1973, beloved Opry performer **David "Stringbean" Akeman** (b. 1916) and his wife Estelle were shot and killed at their home in Ridgetop, Tenn. after they returned from a Saturday night *Opry* performance. Brothers Doug and John Brown had laid in wait for the Akemans, knowing they didn't trust banks and kept large amounts of cash on their person and in their home. The victims were found the next morning by neighbor Grandpa Jones. The Browns were convicted and sentenced to life in prison, where Doug Brown died in 2003. Reportedly, in 1997, $20,000 in rotted cash was found in Stringbean's chimney. Akeman was a banjo picker from Kentucky who used his deadpan comedic delivery and hillbilly costume to entertain audiences. At one time he played semi-pro baseball. He joined the *Opry* in 1942 as part of Bill Monroe's Blue Grass Boys. He also released several solo albums in the 1960s. He was never more popular than at the time of his death. His funeral was attended by the *Opry* greats and 600 mourners. The Akemans are buried at Music Row-10D3 and 10D4.

⑪ **James Phillip Widener** (1918-1973), a rhythm guitar player for Hank Snow's band, was murdered two weeks after the Akeman killings. He was robbed and shot at a downtown motel. A native of Alabama, he was a WWII veteran. (Our Savior-3C1).

① **Grover F. "Big Jeff" Bess** (1920-1998) was the leader of Big Jeff and His Radio Playboys on Nashville radio station WLAC. He recorded for Dot Records. He was married to Tootsie Bess, longtime proprietor of Tootsie's Orchid Lounge downtown on Lower Broadway. Big Jeff Bess played the sheriff in the 1957 movie *A Face in the Crowd*. (Music Row-2B).

② **James C. "Cousin Jody" Summey** (1919-1975). A native of East Tennessee, he performed as a comedian on the Opry, often with Lonzo and Oscar. He was famous for his exaggerated facial expressions, unusual clothes, and dobro guitar playing. Previously, he played dobro for many years with Roy Acuff's Smoky Mountain Boys. In fact, he was the first artist to play dobro on the *Opry* stage, in 1938 at Acuff's audition. (Music Row-8C1).

③ **William O. "Lefty" Frizzell** (1928-1975) was a vocal artist out of Texas and Arkansas who sang with the Western Cherokees on the *Louisiana Hayride* and the Opry. His first single in 1950, "If You've Got the Money, I've Got the Time," went to No. 1. At one time in 1951 he had four songs in the country Top Ten, a record never broken. His last big hit was in 1964 with "Saginaw Michigan." His style influenced many artists, including Merle Haggard and George Jones. He was inducted into the Country Music Hall of Fame in 1982. His younger brother, David, had a series of hits with Shelly West, daughter of Dottie West. (Music Row-8A1).

④ **Judy B. Baker** (1924-2000) was known as Country Music's Hostess (Music Row).

⑨ **Hamilton K. "Smiley" Wilson** (1922-1988) was the leader of the Range Partners, appearing on Shreveport's *Louisiana Hayride*. He also played with the Circle 3 Ranch Gang. A native of Alabama, he was in the 1949 movie *Square Dance Jubilee*. He released the rockabilly "Juke Box Boogie" in 1950. (Masonic).

⑩ **Beecher R. "Bashful Brother Oswald" Kirby** (1911-2002) played dobro many years with Roy Acuff's Smoky Mountain Boys and is considered one of the best dobro players ever. He was also a vocalist and comedic character, wearing an outlandish costume. His stage name of Brother Oswald was a ruse to convince audiences he was related to Acuff's female singer, Rachel Veach, who was not married. He worked as a sessions musician and released several solo albums. (Meditation-152A4).

⑭ **John "Lonzo" Sullivan** (1916-1967). He was the second Lonzo of the *Opry's* hayseed comedy team of Lonzo and Oscar, teaming with brother Rollin Sullivan in 1950 and replacing Lloyd George, the first Lonzo. Johnny had already been a part of the group, which had fronted for Eddy Arnold since 1945. They scored a hit in 1963 called "Country Music Time." Sullivan was killed in a car accident in 1967 and replaced by David Hooten, the third Lonzo. (Last Supper-274B1).

⑮ **Benny E. "Big Tige" Martin** (1928-2001) from Sparta, Tenn. played the fiddle on the *Opry* and toured with many bands, including Monroe's Blue Grass Boys, Scruggs' Foggy Mountain Boys, and Acuff's Smoky Mountain Boys. He also played the eight-string fiddle. He played for Big Jeff Bess and the Radio Playboys and made his *Opry* debut in 1946. (Meditation-9D4).

⑯ **Herman C. Harper** (1938-1993). Deep-voiced singer with the *Opry* backup vocal group The Carol Lee Singers and the Oak Ridge Quartet. He created the Gospel Music Trust Fund and was a leading gospel music talent agent. (Meditation-58C2).

⑱ **Ivan Leroy "Little Roy" Wiggins** (1926-1999). He played distinctive "crying" steel guitar for 25 years in Eddy Arnold's band, the Tennessee Plowboys. He originated the ting-a-ling sound and was noted for his hoy-hoy comedy routine. He also played for George Morgan, the Willis Brothers, and Ernie Ashworth. He was inducted into the Steel Guitar Hall of Fame in 1985. (Gethsemane-150A1).

⑲ **Jimmy Crawford** (1935-2005) was a renowned pedal steel-guitar player, performing with Buck Owens, Johnny Paycheck, Kitty Wells, George Jones, Loretta Lynn, Dolly Parton, Ferlin Huskey, the Osborne Brothers, and many others. He played on the Wheeling (W.Va.) *Jamboree* and the *Grand Ole Opry*. He co-founded the JCH Steel Guitar Company. (Devotion I-28B).

⑳ **Hal Wayne Vest** (1946-2003). He sang, played bass, guitar and drums with Pee Wee King's Golden West Cowboys band and produced Charlie Louvin and Billie Jo Spears. He died in an automobile accident near Nashville. (Mausoleum-25DD).

Luton's United Methodist Church

Louis Marshall "Grandpa" Jones (1913-1998) is buried at Luton's United Methodist Church, 8363 Old Springfield Hwy., in Goodlettsville near the Robertson County line.

Jones was born in Kentucky and was on radio by age 18 as the "Young Singer of Old Songs." His father was a fiddler and his mother sang ballads. In the 1930s he played banjo and toured extensively. He was tagged "Grandpa" by partner Bradley Kincaid because Jones acted "grouchy" during their early-morning radio broadcasts. Jones readily accepted the moniker.

He toured in the 1940s with the Delmore brothers and Merle Travis as the Brown's Ferry Four. He joined the *Grand Ole Opry* in 1946 and became a popular performer there for the rest of his life. He toured with Lonzo and Oscar and Cowboy Copas. His wife Ramona accompanied on fiddle and mandolin. Grandpa Jones became a national television celebrity for his performances on the *Hee Haw* comedy show during the 1970s and 1980s.

Hermitage Memorial Gardens

Hermitage Memorial Gardens is located at 535 Shute Lane in Old Hickory, east of downtown. The phone is (615) 889-0361.

The most famous person buried here is **Ernest Dale Tubb Sr.** (1914-1984), the Texas Troubadour. Tubb was an old-style honky tonk singer and touring star who enjoyed a large, loyal following. He was a member of the *Grand Ole Opry* from 1943 to 1984. He opened the first all-country music store on Lower Broadway where he promoted rising talent on his *Midnight Jamboree* radio show immediately following the Opry on Saturday nights. Tubb also starred in several Hollywood movies. His theme was the million-selling "I'm Walking the Floor Over You." Buried nearby is son **Justin Tubb** (1935-1998), a touring and performing star in his own right.

Also buried here is **Rudolph Walter Wonderon Jr.** (1913-1996), better known as Minnesota Fats, the famous billiards player who resided in his later years at the Hermitage Hotel in downtown Nashville. A pool hustler, he became famous for his televised matches with billiards master Willie Mosconi, whom he never defeated. He was a popular celebrity despite having never won a major billiards tournament. His marker reads "Beat Every Living Creature on Earth. 'St. Peter, Rack 'em Up.' Fats."

Charles R. "Bobby" Hamilton (1957-2007) was a well-known NASCAR race driver. He was NASCAR Rookie of the Year in 1991 and NASCAR Craftsman Truck Series Champion in 2004. He died of cancer at age 49.

Gravesite of Ernest Tubb, with Texas flag.

Rudolph Wonderon, aka Minnesota Fats

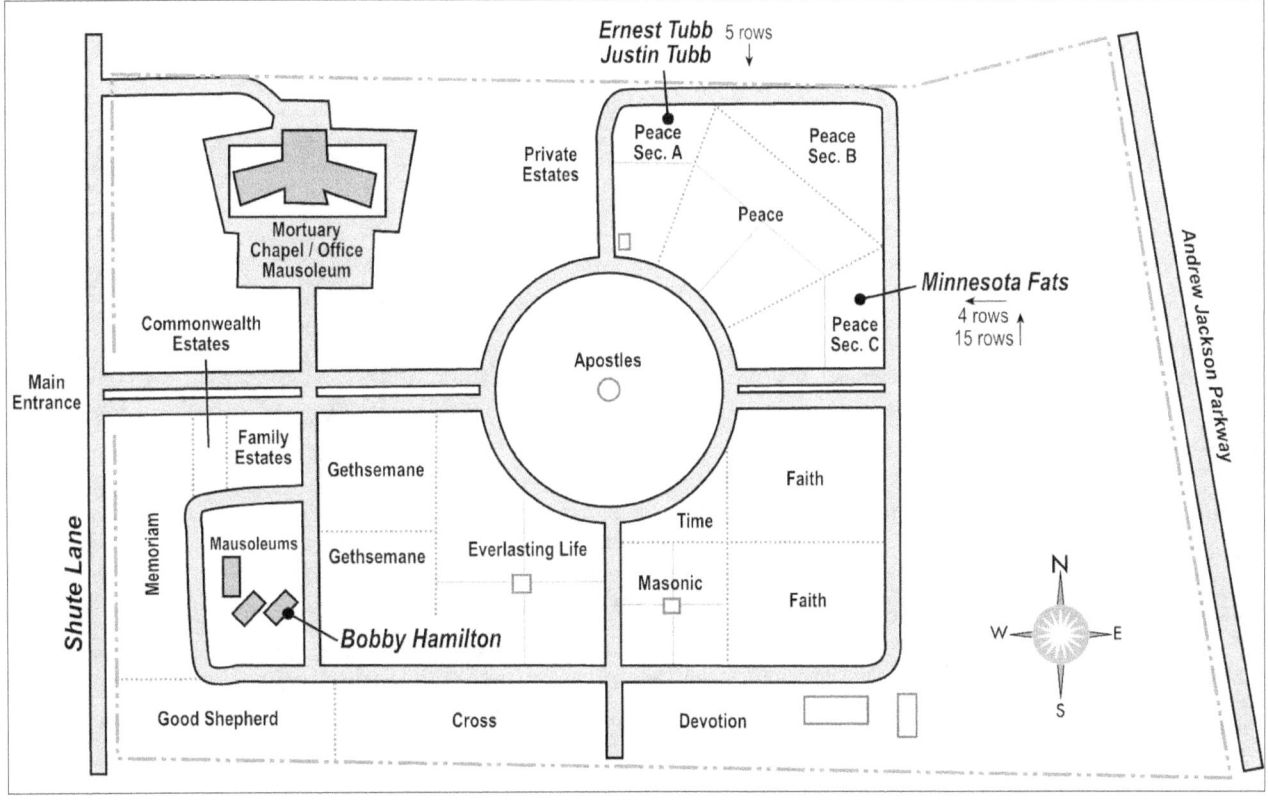

Harpeth Hills Memory Gardens

Harpeth Hills Memory Gardens is located at 9090 Highway 100 (Old Harding Pike) in the far southwestern corner of Davidson County between the intersections with the Natchez Trace Parkway and Highway 96. The phone is 615-646-9292.

Chester Burton "Chet" Atkins (1924-2001) was a talented guitar player and designer, Opry and touring performer, recording artist and record producer, responsible for creating the pop-oriented Nashville Sound in the 1950s and 1960s. A prolific solo artist, Atkins won 11 Grammy awards and nine CMA Instrumentalist of the Year awards.

Born in 1924 in East Tennessee, Atkins began performing as a fiddler, but he earned fame as an accomplished guitar player, imitating the Merle Travis syncopated thumb-and-finger roll. He was hired by radio stations in Cincinnati, Nashville, and Springfield, Mo. to back up artists such as the Carter Sisters and Red Foley during the 1940s. He made his first appearance on the *Grand Ole Opry* in 1946, backing Foley. In 1950 he became a permanent member of the Opry.

In the 1950s Atkins became a well-known studio musician for RCA. He rose up through the ranks, managing RCA's new studio in 1957 and becoming a vice-president in 1968. He produced hits for such stars as Elvis Presley and Eddy Arnold.

As a music producer, Atkins worked with many new stars such as Willie Nelson and Dolly Parton to create a more commercial, accessible, and pop-influenced music known as "The Nashville Sound." As a solo artist, Atkins, known as "Mr. Guitar," recorded many successful albums featuring his unique guitar style. In 1965 he had a hit with "Yakety Axe," a reworking of Boots Randolph's "Yakety Sax." He designed guitars for Gibson and Gretsch. Performing with Homer and Jethro as the Nashville String Band, he released five albums in 1970-72. He retired from RCA in 1981. Recording with the Columbia label, he released several jazz guitar albums. His gravesite is located in the Fountain section.

Brothers **Ira Louvin** (1924-1965), born Lonnie Ira Loudermilk, and **Charlie Louvin** (1927-2011), born Charles Elzer Loudermilk, performed as the Louvin Brothers, a popular *Opry* act from 1955 to 1963, when they broke up to pursue solo careers. Both were inducted into the Country Music Hall of Fame in 2001. Ira played the mandolin and sang with a high tenor voice. He was killed along with his fourth wife in a car crash in Missouri. Charlie died of pancreatic cancer. Both gravesites are located in Everlasting Life section.

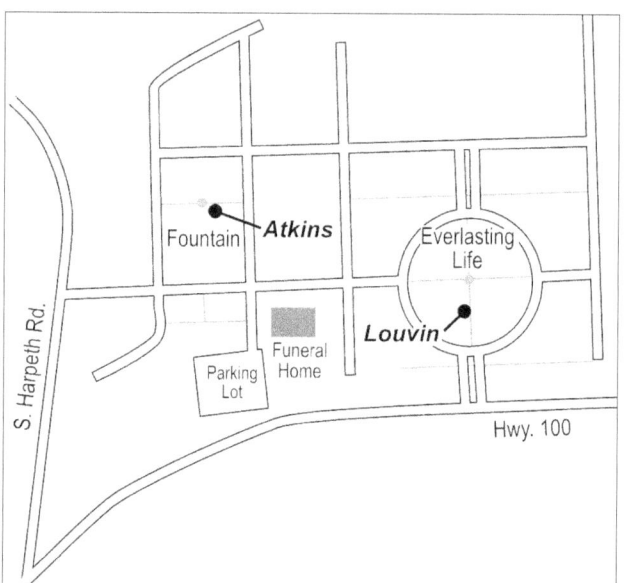

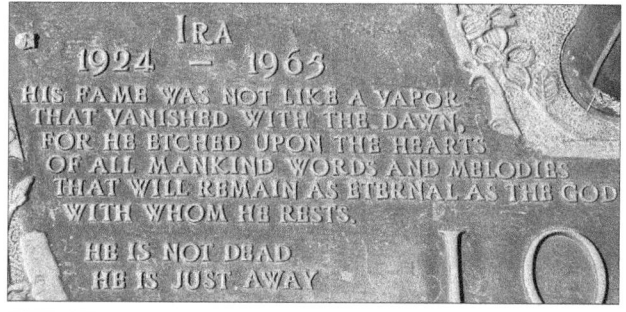

Mount Hope Cemetery, Del Rio Pike, Franklin, Tenn.

Sarah Ophelia Colley Cannon (1912-1996), better known as **Minnie Pearl**, was a beloved country comedian whose "Howdee!" greeting and flowered hat graced the stage of the *Grand Ole Opry* for half a century. Born in Centerville, Tenn., she attended the Ward-Belmont finishing school in Nashville. Her fictional hometown was Grinder's Switch. She also starred on the *Hee Haw* and *Nashville Now* television shows. Offstage she devoted her time and talents to the Vanderbilt Children's Hospital, the National Heart Association, and the American Cancer Society. Nashville's Centennial Medical Center dedicated its cancer center to her. Cannon was inducted into the Country Music Hall of Fame in 1975 and received the National Medal of the Arts in 1991. She is buried at Mount Hope Cemetery in Franklin, Tenn. in Section K.

Williamson Memorial Gardens is located at 3009 Columbia Avenue in Franklin, Tenn. (phone 615-794-2289). Buried here are **Skeeter Davis, Grant Turner, Goldie Hill Smith, Carl Butler, Pearl Butler**, and **Sam** and **Kirk McGee**.

Hendersonville Memory Gardens

Hendersonville Memory Gardens, 353 Johnny Cash Blvd., in Sumner County (615-824-3855) holds the mortal remains of America's country and gospel troubador, Johnny Cash (1932-2003), "The Man in Black," and wife June Carter Cash (1929-2003), along with Mother Maybelle Carter, "The First Lady of Country Music," and the Carter family. Also here are Merle Kilgore, Luther Perkins, Johnny Russell, and Joe Maphis.

Johnny Cash grew up poor in rural Arkansas, served in the U.S. Air Force in Germany, and settled in Memphis with his first wife. Cash recorded with the Tennessee Three (which included Luther Perkins) on Sam Phillips' Sun Records. "I Walk the Line" went No. 1 and sold two million copies. In 1956 he joined the *Grand Ole Opry* and he also appeared on many TV variety shows. In the 1960s he became addicted to drugs and his marriage failed. In 1967, with the help of June Carter, he kicked the habit. The next year they were married. Live albums recorded at Folsom and San Quentin prisons went gold. In 1969 he was CMA's Male Vocalist and Entertainer of the Year. From 1969-1971 he hosted *The Johnny Cash Show* on ABC-TV. He was inducted into the Country Music Hall of Fame in 1980. From 1985 to 1995 he and fellow artists Willie Nelson, Waylon Jennings, and Kris Kristofferson recorded three hit albums as The Highwaymen. In the 1990s Cash recorded a series of Grammy-winning albums on the American Recordings label.

Valerie June Carter was born in Virginia. Her mother was **Maybelle Carter** (1909-1978), who had played country music with her brother-in-law A.P. Carter and his wife Sara. She played guitar, autoharp, and banjo. After The Carters split up, Mother Maybelle began touring and performing with her three daughters, June, **Anita** (1933-1999), and **Helen** (1927-1998), all buried here. A.P. and Sara Carter are buried in Virginia.

June Carter was married in the 1950s to performer Carl Smith. During the 1960s she began performing with Johnny Cash, and married him in 1968. The next year they were voted Vocal Group of the Year. Her 1999 album *Press On* and 2003 album *Wildwood Flower* won a total of three Grammy Awards.

Luther Perkins (1928-1968) was the lead guitarist for Johnny Cash's band from 1955 to 1968, using a style that made all of Cash's songs unique.

Merle Kilgore (1934-2005) was a Nashville Hall of Fame songwriter and the longtime business manager of performer Hank Williams, Jr. He wrote "Ring of Fire" with June Carter Cash. He served on the Board of the Country Music Association.

Otis W. "Joe" Maphis (1921-1986) was a dynamic country guitar player of the 1950s and 1960s, able to play any stringed instrument with agility.

Ferlin Huskey (1925-2011) was inducted into the Country Music Hall of Fame in 2010. He had No. 1 hits with "Gone" and "Wings of a Dove" in the 1950s and created the comedic character of Simon Crum.

Johnny Russell (1940-2001) was a popular member of the Opry beginning in 1985. He sang "Catfish John" and wrote "Act Naturally." He was known for his girth (over 300 lbs.) and his big heart. He is interred in the mausoleum.

Mae Axton (1914-1997) was a songwriter best known for penning "Heartbreak Hotel," a monster hit for Elvis Presley. She is interred in the mausoleum.

Sheb Wooley (1921-2003), a songwriter who wrote "Purple People Eater" and "High Noon," died days after attending Johnny Cash's funeral. He is interred in the mausoleum.

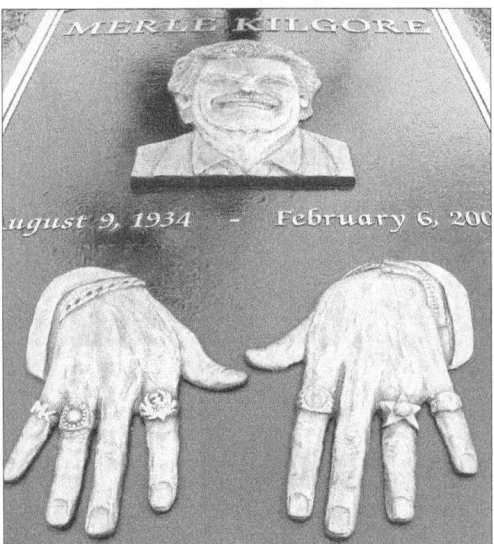

Index of Names
Personages Listed in the Historic Cemeteries

A
Acklen, Adelicia 23
Acuff, Roy 48
Akeman, David 61
Akeman, Stringbean 61
Anderson, Samuel Read 13
Armstrong, Robert 17
Arnold, Eddy 57
Arnold, Richard Edward 57
Atkins, Chester Burton 64
Atkins, Chet 64
Axton, Mae 65

B
Bader, Herman 41
Bailey, Deford 34
Baker, Judy B. 61
Bashful Brother Oswald 62
Bate, William Brimage 25
Baxter, Robert 15
Beall, William N.R. 25
Bell, John 23
Bess, Big Jeff 61
Bess, Grover F. 61
Bierfield, S.A. 36
Biggs, Bunny 50
Biggs, David M. 50
Big Howdy 50
Bloomstein, Judah 36
Boyd, Henry A. 34
Boyd, Richard H. 34
Boyd, Robert Fulton 33
Bradford, John 13, 15
Bradley, William Owen 57
Briley, Clifton Beverly 52
Brown, Aaron V. 27
Brown, Alex C. 17
Brown, Lizinka Campbell 15
Bryan, Josephine 13
Bryan, Mary Cannon 13
Bryant, Boudleaux 55
Bryant, Felice 55
Bryan, W.P. 13

C
Campbell, George Washington 15
Cannon, Newton 13
Cannon, Sarah Ophelia Colley 64
Cantrell, Charles 41, 42
Carr, John 41, 42
Carroll, William 13
Carson, Martha 59
Carter, Anita 65
Carter, Daniel F. 25
Carter, Helen 65
Carter, Maybelle 65
Carter, Mother Maybelle 65

Carter, Valerie June 65
Cash, Johnny 65
Cash, June Carter 65
Catron, John 27
Chapman, Samuel 13
Cheatham, Benjamin F. 25
Claiborne, Thomas 15
Cockrill, Ann Robertson Johnston 19
Cockrill, John 13, 17
Cole, Edmund W. 23
Coleman, Joseph 13
Coleman, Thomas 13
Cooper, Dale T. 58
Cooper, Stoney 58
Copas, Cowboy 61
Copas, Lloyd E. 61
Cousin Jody 61
Cowboy Copas 61
Craighead, Thomas B. 53
Cravath, Erastus M. 41
Crawford, Jimmy 62
Curran, Robert P. 15

D
Dallas, Ella 19
Davis, Mary Reeves 50
Drake, Pete 50
Driver, William 17
Dudley, Anne Dallas 29

E
Elliott, C.D. 15
Ewell, Richard 15

F
Fanning, Tolbert 30
Fisk Jubilee Singers 34
Fogg, Francis 15
Fogg, Mary Rutledge 15
Foley, Clyde J. 59
Foley, Red 59
Forrester, Howard 50
Fort, Cornelia Clark 30
Foster, Anthony 13
Foster, Bob 61
Foster, Ephraim 19
Foster, Robert L. 61
Freehan, Patrick A. 32
Frizzell, Lefty 61
Frizzell, William O. 61
Furman, Francis 27
Furman, Mary J. 27

G
Gallant, Ralph 59
Gentry, Meredith Poindexter 23
Gibson, Curt 50

Gillem, Alvan C. 25
Gilliam, Joe Jr. 34
Grundy, Felix 23
Grundy, Louisa Caroline 27

H
Hagey, John E. 17
Hamilton, Bobby 63
Hamilton, Charles R. 63
Harding, John 25
Harding, William Giles 25
Harper, Herman C. 62
Hartford, John 52
Hawkins, Hankshaw 61
Hawkins, Harold F. 61
Hayes, Oliver B. 27
Heiman, Adolphus 13, 23
Herman, Benjamin 36
Hill, H.G. 30
Hill, Horace Greeley 30
Hill, J.D. 13
Howard, Harlan 19
Howard, Jan 19
Howell, Robert Boyte Crawford 27
Hume, Alfred 15
Hume, William 15
Huskey, Ferlin 65
Huskey, Roy M. 50

I
Imes, Mable Lewis 19
Inman, Robert Autry 61

J
Jackson, Andrew 4
Jackson, Howell E. 25
Jackson, Rachel 4
Jackson, Red 23
Jackson, Thomas Lee 58
Jackson, Tommy 58
Jackson, William Hicks 23
Jamup 50
Jefferson Street Joe 34
Johnson, Bushrod Rust 13
Johnson, W.A. 15
Johnston, Ann Robertson 17
Jones, Edward . 41
Jones, Grandpa 62
Jones, Louis Marshall 62

K
Kane, John 13
Kelley, David C. 23
Kilgore, Merle 65
Kirby, Beecher R. 62
Kirk, Pamelia A. 13
Kornman-Raskin 36

L
Lavender, Grover C. 59
Lavender, Shorty 59
Lawless, James W. 41
Lea, Luke 25
Leonard, James A. 41
Lettman, Julius 36
Levy, Zadoc 36
Lewis, Eugene C. 27
Lewis, Joel 13
Lindsley, John Berrien 27
Lindsley, Philip 27
Lipscomb, David 30
Londin, Larrie 59
Louvin, Charlie 64
Louvin, Ira 64
Love, Richard 19
Lowenheim, Joseph 36
Lucas, Charles 53
Lucas, Red 53
Lyell, William 41
Lyell, William F. 42
Lytle, Donald E. 57

M
Maddis, Charles 13
Maney, George E. 25
Mansker, Kasper 7
Manuel, Dockie Dean 52
Maphis, Joe 65
Maphis, Otis W. 65
Mariah, Anna 19
Marlin, Archibald 13
Marlin, Dan 13
Marlin, Henry 13
Martin, Benny E. 62
Martin, Big Tige 62
Martin, Jimmy 48
Maynor, Nancy 13
Maynor, Pleasant 13
McAlister, Hill 27
McAlister, William King 27
McGavock, Jacob 27
McNairy, John 15
Merritt, John A. 34
Middleton, Septima Sexta 15
Minnesota Fats 63
Minnie Pearl 64
Mitchell, Jacob 36
Monroe, Bill 50
Moore, Ella Shepherd 17
Morgan, George T. 50
Morton, John W. 25

N
Nichol, Margaret 17
Norvell, Lipscomb 13

O
Orbison, Anthony King 55
Orbison, Claudette 55
Orbison, Roy Dewayne 55
Overton, John 27

P
Patterson, West 41
Paycheck, Johnny 57
PayCheck, Johnny 57
Peabody, John 19
Perkins, Luther 65
Pierce, Webb 59
Polk, James K. 6
Polk, Sarah Childress 6

R
Rains, James 13
Rains, James E. 23
Reed, William R. 34
Rhodes, Gilbert Speck 50
Ridley, George 37
Ridley, Sarah 37
Rivers, Burrhead 53
Rivers, Gerald M. 53
Rivers, Jerry 53
Robbins, Marty 59
Robertson, Charlotte 15
Robertson, Duncan 17
Robertson, Felix 15
Robertson, James 15
Rood, Oliver P. 26
Rose, Fred 30
Russell, Johnny 65
Rutledge, Henry 15
Rutledge, Mary 15
Ryman, Thomas Green 29

S
Salzkotter, Felix 36
Sanders, Ann Rawlins 13
Sanders, Charles 13
Scruggs, Earl 48
Sevier, John 15
Shelby, John 19
Shelby, Sarah Bledsoe 19
Shirley, Paul 17
Smith, Feedrick 19
Smith, Kelly Miller 34
Smith, Sam G. 17
Smith, Thomas Benton 23
Snow, Clarence 50
Snow, Hank 50
Sovine, Red 55
Sovine, Woodrow Wilson 55
Speer, Jackson Brock 55
Stapp, Jack 55
Steele, Edward 13
Stephenson, Van 55
Stevenson, Vernon K. 29
Stoneman, Calvin S. 30
Stoneman, Ernest Van 30
Stoneman, Harriet F. 30
Stoneman, Hattie 30
Stoneman, Jimmy 30
Stoneman, Oscar J. 30
Stoneman, Pop 30
Stoneman, Scotty 30
Stoneman, Van Haden 30

Stratton, Madison 53
Stratton, Thomas 53
Street, Mel 59
Stringbean 61
Sullivan, John 62
Sullivan, Lonzo 62
Summey, James C. 61
Sumner, J.D. 55
Sumner, John Daniel 55

T
Tannehill, Wilkins 17
Taylor, Preston 34
Thompson, Hugh Cathcart 29
Thruston, Gates P. 25
Troost, Gerard 19
Tubb, Ernest Dale 63
Tubb, Justin 63
Turpin, White 19

U
Uncle Billy 34

V
Van Leer, Anthony Wayne 25
Vest, Hal Wayne 62
Vickery, Willard Mack 59

W
Wagoner, Porter 58
Walker, Billy 50
Walker, John W. 13
Walker, Sarah Ann Gray 13
Warner, Edwin 30
Warner, Katharine Burch 29
Warner, Leslie 29
Warner, Percy 27
Waters, Lydia 15
Watkins, Samuel 27
West, Ben 13
West, William Edward 15
White, Granny 7
White, Lucinda Wilson 7
Whitley, Keith 52
Whitson, Beth Slater 53
Whyte, Robert 13
Widener, James Phillip 61
Wiggins, Little Roy 62
Wiggins, Roy 62
Willis, John Victor 59
Willis, Vic 59
Wilson, Hamilton K. 61
Wilson, Smiley 61
Wonderon, Rudolph Walter 63
Wooley, Sheb 65
Wynette, Tammy 55

Z
Zollicoffer, Felix 17

www.ingramcontent.com/pod-product-compliance
Lightning Source LLC
Chambersburg PA
CBHW080520300426
44112CB00018B/2810